MW00890878

All in Good Time

Life Stories
Grown From
Southern Roots

LANE ALDRIDGE

OUTER BANKS PRESS

All in Good Time
Life Stories Grown From Southern Roots

FIRST EDITION

Copyright © 2017 Lane Aldridge

All rights reserved.
No part of this publication may be reproduced,
stored in a retrieval system, or transmitted in any
form or by any means, without express written
permission from the author or publisher.

Library of Congress Cataloguing-in-Publication
data available upon request.

Published by Outer Banks Press

Book editing and design:
Linda L. Lauby, Outer Banks Press

Outer Banks Press
P.O. Box 2829
Kitty Hawk, NC 27949
outerbankspress.com | info@outerbankspress.com
252.261.0612

For Hannah and Adam

Acknowledgments

"Much Obliged, Folks"

I don't remember ever hearing my daddy say "thank you." Oh, not that he was ungrateful – Daddy said "much obliged" – and I think that is a really serious thank you.

So here I sit, on the fifteenth of May 2017, at the end of about ten years of writing on and off and, believe me, I am much obliged to a lot of people for seeing me through this – well, I started to say this *project*, then *effort*, but what it's been is a *journey*.

There have been writer friends who early on read a few stories and gave me valuable feedback, mainly and in order, Suzanne Kingsbury, Ginia Desmond, Debra Sanders, Janet Parks. Some of the stories had their start through posts on Facebook, and many friends there, some writers themselves, some not, gave me encouragement to keep going. Close friends Sandy Treadwell and Pat Keeler and Joanne Ferguson have been boosters to keep the keyboard fires burning.

My sister – Lori Aldridge-Love – and I are practically a generation apart, and we each had our own versions of growing up on the farm, of time spent at Grandma

Helms's house; some of these stories we lived together, and she was invaluable as a fact-checker. My brother-in-law, Jim Love, a wonderful writer himself, graciously volunteered to be a reader for me. Hannah Lane Love and Adam Love – my niece and nephew – don't even know their primary role in the writing of this book: when I realized they never got to experience what life had been like for their mom and me at Grandma's house, that's when I knew I had to share those memories with them. Ellen Upchurch and Joan Helms, sisters who were my best buddies growing up, encouraged my writing. My regret is that Joanie died this year before getting to see the book finished; she had so looked forward to reading it.

And then there is the incomparable and multitalented Linda L. Lauby. She's a writer, an editor, a publisher, an artist, a photographer, a resident lover of my beloved Outer Banks of North Carolina, and devoted dog-mama to some of the most gorgeous creatures you'd ever want to set eyes on. We barely knew each other on Facebook, and I had no idea she had been reading the few things I had posted. Out of the blue one day, she said my stories needed "to be out there," and offered to be my editor. I promise you, she's been my manna from heaven! You would not be reading this were it not for her keen eye and knowledge.

To all of you who have helped me, to all of you who have read my stories, and to you who are about to read them, I am truly much obliged.

Contents

Foreword

Every now and then, a book comes along that is so rich, so vivid in its description of characters and setting, that it transports you to another time and place, leaving you with the odd feeling you've somehow been an active part of that writer's journey and experiences. There are a handful of writers who have accomplished this, and now, with **All in Good Time**, Lane Aldridge can be added to that group of authors who enrich our lives simply by virtue of sharing theirs.

I have both read and listened to the essays in this volume. Many I have listened to and/or read multiple times, for the sheer enjoyment of them. And whether I closed the book, or turned off the audio, I've consistently walked away with the word rich ringing in my mind. The characters are rich. The language Aldridge uses is rich. The experiences themselves are rich.

When one thinks about what traits all the best Southern writers share, certain elements come to mind. Among them is a celebration of eccentricity, a sense of humor in the face of adversity, and an enduring and unbreakable connection to both family and place. Well, in this collection of essays about growing up in the South, Aldridge delivers on all counts.

Whether you are reading about the terror of Christmas Eve when twelve-year-old Aldridge is hiding in a bathtub with her mother while a crazed townsperson is trying to shoot the door open, or laughing over Grandma Aldridge's unique take on cats, and Daddy's interesting way of cussing, each story leaves you with such a rich (there's that word again) understanding of the South in the years before the advent of cell phones and Internet.

Each one of Aldridge's stories, whether humorous or profound (and many are both), is filled with language that reads with a cadence, a rhythm, and with such command of the nuances of language, that whether you are hearing or reading them, you are left with the feeling that you've just sat around one of those big, round Southern kitchen tables and listened to her spin you a tale about growing up.

I can't think of a better way to spend an afternoon and evening.

~ Debra Sanders, author of the bestselling memoir **A Matter of Panache.**

Introduction

A few months shy of my sixty-fifth birthday I
was helping a friend organize notes for her novel.
When we worked together, we talked. And when we
talked, we laughed. A lot. We swapped stories – of
her Jewish childhood in upstate New York, of mine
on a Southern farm. Our bartering and bantering
gave birth to these stories you are about to read:
our laughter helped me to re-appreciate people
and places and moments I have too often taken for
granted, and it was what made me decide to write
down some of the memories that warm my heart,
that make me laugh, that make me sad. Not sure
exactly why I felt the compulsion to begin writing,
but it seemed to me the thing to do at this stage of
my life. And perhaps it has something to do with
the mathematical fact that now, at my age, time is
spinning under me, faster than ever.

You see, time is a relative thing. Long ago I heard a
reasonable explanation for why time seems to drag
for children and speed up as one ages. Here's how
the phenomenon was described to me. Imagine
you're ten years old, your birthday just passed, you
got some great gifts, and you are already thinking
of what you think you want for your next birthday.

(We're just pretending that you're Greedy Gus, okay?) You soon begin to think your next special day is never going to come because a whole year takes forever. And it is a long time – relatively speaking. Relative to your particular ten-year life on this planet, a year is a whole 10 percent of your entire time here. But one day you become fifty years old, and one year is only 2 percent of your life; 2 percent of your lifetime seems to pass much more quickly than 10 percent. That made perfect sense to me. So I guess I felt I had to write before I ran out of percentage.

No one ever gave me a formula for the relativity of memory. I know it's a tricky thing, memory. It's affected by time, affected by health, affected by ob-servation, by interest, even by beliefs. What we care about most – whether we weigh it as fortunate or not – we're likely to remember the longest: emotion is the oil that lubricates memory. Yet that's not to say we're guaranteed to remember any event, any place, anybody the same as someone who shared those experiences with us. Natalie Goldberg says one must come at memoir by a side door, but I didn't read that until after I had peeked through a window, a window that opened into a room of my own making, decorated with the pictures, the furnishings, the activities of my own life, my own choices – perhaps some choices that I didn't think were mine at the time. The room may appear to be filled with past, present, and hints of future, but those are all illusions, aren't they? Any memory, after all, is only a fact of the moment, it's not the experience itself. I do not make promises of pure accuracy here, but I do promise honesty.

I admit you will come across some repetition, partly because the stories were written to stand alone rather than strictly to fit the chronology of my life. Therefore, you may, for example, be "introduced" to a person or a job more than once.

Whatever else it may be, this exercise, this effort, this commitment to write down the stories began as an attempt to record memories that scramble through my mind: to consider each experience as it replays itself there; to smile again at faces long gone, some forever and permanently; even to smile at the backs of some heads as they moved on, thankfully, out of my life. Truth be told, this writing was the most fun I've had in a very long time, not always easy, not polished, but always satisfying. Perhaps writing has helped me make just a wee bit of sense out of this one particular life – the one that has been mine to live – one that could've been better or worse but wasn't, one that on some days felt wasted, but on many days has felt as magical as it truly, and wholly, has been.

I hope that sharing my recollections will offer you a chuckle now and then as well as an occasional something that will stir a memory or two of your own. Maybe you, along with me, will remember that we all have experienced some measure of joy within our days that stumble along, gradually collecting themselves and, finally at the end, culminate in a word we call Life.

Chapter 1

My Name's Not Lane

I wasn't born with the name Lane. In fact, it's a wonder I was born at all. I know – the birth of any baby is considered a miracle, but not only was I not "Lane," I didn't start out as a baby, either. I was a tumor.

Mama and Daddy had been married for nine barren years, all the while praying for a child, when finally one day Mama realized she must be pregnant. She made an appointment and the doctor ordered tests: the rabbit test, the frog test. That's what they did back then to see if a woman was indeed pregnant. In old movies, you might see a husband come home from work and when he comes through the door, his wife runs to meet him and excitedly reports, "The rabbit died!" It had become a euphemism for "I'm pregnant!"

The rabbit test was pretty self-explanatory: urine from the woman in question was injected into a rabbit, then the rabbit was killed, and her ovaries were examined for something called hCG – a peptide hormone produced by the human fetus soon after conception and by the placenta later on. If hCG was present in Little Rabbit Fru-Fru's ovaries, Mama was pregnant. Now, this could have been done without killing the rabbit, but it would've been more time-consuming and expensive, so, of course, they chose to kill the rabbit. The rabbit always died, having been injected with pregnant-pee or not, 'cause they killed it, but the euphemism was needed anyway, for "pregnancy" was almost a dirty word.

Whatever and what all they could do in 1942 to determine the validity of my mama's assumption that she was pregnant, they did do. All negative. Three different trips she made to Doctor Monroe's office, telling him that she knew she was pregnant, and every time, this man sent her home, telling her no, she wasn't.

Mama had had a variety of problems "down there" – another one of those useful euphemisms. She had been born with only one ovary and her womb was "upside down" (which must have been the description back then of a tilted uterus). Among her "female problems" was a history of fibroid tumors and already a few surgeries to get rid of them. So here she was, feeling totally sure that she was pregnant, and this doctor was sending her home after a physical examination with one more "no," although with some additional news.

"But there is a growth; it's a tumor and it must come out."

He scheduled surgery. Because of Mama's medical history, the doctor considered this a serious procedure and asked Daddy to wait outside the operating room door.

Twenty years later, Daddy told us the rest of the story. He said that Mama hadn't been in surgery long when Doctor Monroe burst through the doors "white as a ghost and with eyes big as saucers."

"Mr. Aldridge, I've operated on your wife and found a pregnancy. What do you want me to do?"

"What do you mean, what do I want you to do?"

"Do you want me to abort or sew her back up? Your wife is going to be okay either way, but nine chances out of ten, the baby won't live – and if it does, it won't be normal." (I have friends who think that explains a lot!)

Daddy said, "Sew her back up. And don't tell her any of this."

Years later, when Daddy told what had happened that day to a first-time mother and a three-month fetus, he also said that the next six months were agony for him. After Mama would fall asleep at night, he'd lay his hand on her belly and he wouldn't feel the baby move. He'd think, *It's dead*, or *It doesn't have any legs*.

Mama had to stay in bed almost constantly those next six months. She underwent surgery again the day before Thanksgiving, only this time she came home with me, Carol Elaine Aldridge. As if being a tumor wasn't enough, I was almost a turkey.

Seventeen years later, and after several more surgeries

for actual tumors, once again Mama thought she was pregnant. And she was. When Lori was born, Mama was forty-four, Daddy was forty-six, and I was seventeen, one month away from high school graduation. Daddy had had grey hair since his thirties and strangers were forever telling him what a beautiful granddaughter he had. He corrected them quickly and proudly.

Three years after Lori joined us, Mama had been having so many problems "down there" again, that she had to have a hysterectomy. Only after that did Daddy reveal to us the secret held by him, Doctor Monroe, and that operating room twenty years before. His rationale for never having told Mama what had happened was that, just in case she might become pregnant again, he didn't want her to worry.

~April 25, 2008~

Chapter 2

Growin' Up on Kerr Street

As a small child with my head resting on her smooshy breasts, I was in the safest nest I ever knew. I have no memory of a similar experience with my mother. Zella Mae Helms was a formidable woman; those "pillows" were the only soft things about Grandma Helms, because her five-foot-ten-inch frame carried over three hundred pounds, the mid-section of them being encased by a rock-hard corset with a skeleton of innumerable staves. Seeing one of her corsets hanging to dry on laundry day struck me as being a fabric prison waiting to surround my grandmother once again. I have pictures of her outdoors, in a winter coat and hat, but I never saw her in real life in any garment other than a homemade housedress, usually covered by a full length over-the-neck apron, because Grandma spent most of her time in her kitchen. HER kitchen! Five months after Mama died in 1975, Grandma followed her, a little more than two months before my Aunt Dorothy turned fifty. Even though her name was Dorothy, we always called her Toonsie, and she and Grandma shared that house – on Grandma's terms, of course – until Grandma died. A year later,

Toonsie married Joe Rabon, a man of simple mind and gentle heart whom she had dated for twenty-five years.

Grandma did the all the cooking and Toonsie washed the dishes, except when some of the rest of us were eating there too, which was most of the time, and then we all pitched in for the cleanup. Toonsie offered to help with meals but Grandma told her to get out of the kitchen, as she didn't know how to cook. And she didn't, because Grandma never taught her. She managed to observe enough, I reckon, to keep herself and Joe from starving to death after they married, and most of it was palatable so long as she didn't pepper everything the way she preferred it on her own plate: black!

Childhood memories tend to lump themselves into categories, and I have a lump of time-at-Grandma's memories as big as the woman herself, most of which involve food. Grandma was a great cook – not in a gourmet way, mind you, but in the traditional Southern cooking way: meat and green vegetables always graced the table, accompanied by an ample number of white things – potatoes or rice or those god-awful giant white lima beans and bread. Soft white bread – homemade biscuits or rolls or "light bread" from a loaf of Sunbeam, but never any of that hard-crust-soft-center Yankee bread that I still have not learned to like, let alone prefer. The hardest bread that might show up on Grandma's table was a basket of over-baked canned biscuits after Pillsbury pretended to do American families a favor by coming up with them. Grandma did let Toonsie bake them, and that might be why they turned up hard in the basket. Sometimes, Grandma would work a little of her magic for us grandkids by pinching those raw plastic biscuits apart, shaping the pieces into little torpedoes, rolling them in sugar and cinnamon, and baking them. We hung around the oven door as eager as rapt children at story time.

Grandpa Helms was a wretch of an old man with a generous dose of unkindness meted out to everyone around him. The family loved playing dominoes, and while Grandpa demanded strict silence during his turn at play, during everyone else's he would incessantly tap his fingertips on the table. I have a few memories of him after his stroke, when he became even more cantankerous. He would sit in his rocker in the corner of the sitting room, beside the only heater in the house, and even when he was staring in silence, his nasty spirit was almost audible. He and Grandma had a tiny white and brown terrier named Davy. Apparently Grandpa's false teeth hurt him a lot, and that really pissed him off; more than once he was known to take out his teeth, fling them across the room, and no matter where they landed, Davy would go get them and happily take them back to Grandpa. When Grandpa had his final stroke and spent his last days in the back bedroom, Davy lay under his bed the entire time and didn't come out, even to eat.

As strong as these memories are, one of the most vivid is of my Grandpa in his casket in the front room of the house. That's what folks did back then:

someone would die, they would lie in state at home, and friends and relatives would come by to pay their last respects. In his case, I think people came out of respect for the family, because I never heard of much reason for Grandpa to deserve it for himself. I was less than five years old at the time, and he was the first dead person I ever saw, for real, but near the casket hung the large-as-life black-and-white photograph of my handsome, mustached and uni-formed Uncle Lewis who taught me to love banana sandwiches. But then Lewis went away to fight in World War II and never came home. Even at such a young age, I think I sensed that room as a gallery of death, and for years following that day I would think I'd catch a lingering whiff of funeral bouquets as I passed through from the front door on my way to Grandma's kitchen.

Lewis had been the middle child of seven; when he died, six siblings remained. My daddy's side of the family didn't corner the market on nicknames: on Mama's side there were Wallace (known as Jack, married to Odessa/Deck); Olin (Mutt); Burdette (Dette or A. B., for Alan Burdette, and married to Orine/Ikey); Willie Mae, my mother (Hickie, married to Luther/Buddy); Dorothy (Toonsie); and Harold, who, for the most part, maintained his actual name. Once in a while someone would address him by his nickname, "Dooky," but since that was a euphemism for poop, using it was dis-couraged. The origins of most of these nicknames are unknown to me, but I did hear that Mama's uncle was responsible for hers: when she was a new-born and he first saw her, he said, "Well, ain't she a cute little doohicky!" By the time Grandpa died, all the children were married except for Toonsie and Harold, and Harold had begun or was about to begin his religious career by attending L.I.F.E. Bible College in Los Angeles. He was headed to class one day and as he rounded the corner of a building, he literally bumped into a quick-witted student who, when bouncing back from the impact, pulled two make-believe pistols from her imaginary holsters and said, "Twuh! Twuh!" shooting him twice. That's the day she was dubbed "Twogun," but as their work in the church grew, we retrained ourselves to try to call her Winona. They've been married more than seventy years now.

My cousins who lived close enough to Grandma's house for us to play (and eat!) there were Joanie and Ellen, who belonged to Dette and Orine, and George and Danny (Diana), Jack's and Deck's kids. I was closest in age to Joanie and Ellen, and we spent many an hour playing house and school under the canopy of the giant fig tree outside the sitting room window. Fifty years later when I was finally able to buy my own house, the deciding factor was a fig tree outside its dining room window.

Southern summers can be ungodly hot and humid; sometimes I'd be afraid to look down, for fear I'd find out I'd melted into a puddle. For kids especially, there was a direct correlation between heat and humidity and the boredom that naturally came with it, and as anybody knows, boredom can breed trouble. One especially nasty day, Joanie and I were bored senseless. A large rubber tree plant stood in a pot by

Grandma's front door, and she had mothered that sucker until it was taller than we were. Its spiraling, leathery leaves were managing the heat much better than Joanie and I were, but they were in the way of our urgent plan. We methodically stripped off every one of them, as if wishing on a daisy for Mother Nature to show us a little more love and mercy. Once there was nothing left but a naked rod of green flesh, we stepped into the pot. We held on to each other's arms to keep our balance, and walked 'round and 'round in the rich dirt, cooling off and singing to our hearts' – and feet's – content. The singing was what brought Grandma to the porch, but the unexpected sight of what used to be her precious plant was what grabbed her attention. For a split second, I thought her face was red because she was as hot as we had been, but no: it was the only time she ever threatened to spank me.

Perhaps in those houses on Concord's North Union Street where the fancier families lived it might have been different, but with families like ours, there was no such thing as dinner on any weekday, only breakfast, lunch and supper. Sunday was different: the midday meal, the one right after Sunday morning preaching let out, was called Sunday dinner. It was not unusual for any or all of these aunts, uncles, and cousins to be at Grandma's for supper any evening or for dinner on Sunday. Neither was it unusual for any one of Grandma's children to invite somebody from church to "come on over to the house" at mealtime. Grandma and Toonsie were poor as church mice, but somehow Grandma always managed to have a table full of food, and she could pull enough extras out of somewhere to stretch the meal to fit the number of people who had come to be fed – more of her magic. I always thought she was just as good as Jesus with his loaves and fishes.

Grandma didn't go to church, said she didn't need to be in the building to be in church. I'm sure she meant what she said, and perhaps I learned that from her, but the rest of the truth was that it was very hard for her to travel – to get dressed up, get down the steps, into a car, and sit that long on a pew. Once our church, "the Lighthouse," started broadcasting the Sunday morning service, she usually listened to it on the radio that sat on top of the refrigerator while she was cooking Sunday dinner, in preparation for her family and guests, expected and unexpected, to arrive.

When Grandma Helms sat, she sat in her La-Z-Boy Recliner, relaxing with a dip of Peach Sweet Snuff. There was always a tin can on the floor beside her chair, until years later when I bought her a brass spittoon. She did love her snuff!

There was not one bit of foolishness about Grandma Helms, nor did she tolerate much silliness. I don't remember her at all as someone who joked; she actually didn't even talk very much, but when she did, she said exactly what she thought, no matter what, flat out honest and straight. I'm not implying that she was mean or that she didn't have a sense of humor; she did, but I never heard her laugh, really laugh. God knows her house was FULL of laughter, so much so that the memory of family time there is the single most precious thing about my childhood, never to be topped until I was seventeen and my sister Lori's birth outranked it. Daddy once got so tickled at one of my uncles that he slid right off Grandma's blue vinyl couch, onto the floor, laughing so hard I really thought he was going to die. We might see Grandma's belly shake a bit, as much as it could behind that corset, or hear an easy "hmph" from her, but more than likely the most she would evidence was a slight smile or a twinkle in her eyes.

Grandma Helms was a creator – with her family, with her garden, with her cooking, and she was a natural artist. I would give just about anything to have one of the old cheap metal, scalloped serving trays that she decorated. She would paint the ugly old things black and then add an assortment of roses and other flowers around the edges, and the trays would come to life. When the time came that I painted on canvases or signs and especially when I taught tole painting, I would think of Grandma. I appreciated and demanded the best possible brush for the task at hand, and I cared for each one as if it were gold. Tole painting was what Grandma had done, whether she knew to call it that or not, and I wonder to this day how she did what she did with a stiff, scrubby brush that couldn't possibly come to a point. She even loved Paint-By-Number kits when they became available; she painted **Blue Boy** and **Pinkie**, dogs, horses and farm scenes with great care, and could even make some of them look like they weren't paint-by-number. I do have a few of those, but oh, those trays. ... Sometimes she "took in sewing" when someone wanted a dress made, the only way I ever knew her to earn any money, and I guess it was another creative outlet for her, if also a necessity.

Nothing about Elvis Presley squared with our church doctrine, least of all his gyrations, so a lot of people we associated with – meaning family, and "family" meaning Foursquare (our church) – did not approve of him. Except for Grandma, that is, who absolutely adored everything about the man. Before he appeared in our lives, her kids had pitched in and bought Grandma a TV set, rabbit ears and all. On Sunday nights, she made sure she was planted straight in front of the TV, firmly in her easy chair with her spit-can by her side, whenever Ed Sullivan was about to come on – in case Elvis would be on the show. She watched him; I watched her. Her expression – one of tenderness – was reserved for Elvis. She had no time for putting up with criticism about him.

"I don't know why people don't just leave him alone," she'd say, "he's a good boy!"

There were two stores near Grandma's house. Joe Williams, surely one of the nicest men who ever lived, had a service station catty-cornered across the street. If Joe had been a character in one of my favorite comic books back then, the artist would have given him black hair with blue highlights, used ample ink to incise the deep, parenthetical smile lines, and would've added a gleam to his toothy smile to match the twinkle in his eye. Joe's sort of place has become simply a "gas station" today, but back then, one got more than gas when filling the tank: Joe would come out the door, smiling and whistling, both at once (not a particularly easy feat), lower the license plate where the gas pipe was hidden, insert the nozzle, and busy himself washing all the windows and windshield and checking the oil and hoses and belts, offering his assessment of their quality before the tank was filled. There was no automatic cut-off back then, and Joe had his timing down to a science to finish all his kindness and still avoid a spill.

Just inside the front door and backed up against Joe's counter was a wide, red, refrigerated box where "drinks" were kept cold standing in the bottom of the box. Generally speaking, in the South, anything that was a soft drink was generically referred to as "a drink" or even "a Coke," regardless of brand. "Going to Joe's" was how we cousins learned to look both ways before crossing the street, where we learned to pay and get change, where we learned everyday lessons in kindness, and, eventually, that the memory of Joe's smiles and greetings was much greater refreshment than all the five-cent drinks we bought from him. Whenever he saw us running across the street toward him or bounding into his store, it was "Hi, Sissy!" no matter which one of us was there or even if we all three went in. Joe's drink box was temporary home to ice-cold bottles of Coca-Cola, Pepsi, NeHi Grape, Orange Crush, RC, A&W Root Beer, and others. I was a Pepsi kid, except when there was a Cheerwine in the icebox. Cheerwine is a soft drink that for years was peculiar only to the Piedmont area of North Carolina, being bottled in Salisbury, about twenty miles from Concord. (Now, almost a hundred years after its inception and with recent advanced marketing, it can be found in specialty beverage stores here in Tucson. Why, the company's website says Cheerwine is "regularly spotted in such faraway places as the great wall of China, the fjords of Northern Europe, and the battlefields of Iraq." It's not really a wine; it was named Cheerwine because of its burgundy wine color and its cheery bubbles. The original flavoring was uniquely cherry although it was derived from the oil of almonds, of all things, and that made it taste sweeter than other soft drinks but with less sugar, although we didn't know to pay attention to such things back then, let alone care. Deee-licious stuff! So, Joanie and Ellen and I would beg nickels from any adults who were present and run across the street to Joe's to get our treats – sometimes a Coke and a bag of salted peanuts to pour into the Coke to make it fizz and taste salty – and return to Grand-ma's swing to bask in our sugary pleasures.

Two doors down from Grandma's house was Ruby Furr's grocery store, a large, two-story clapboard building in dull, dirty grey. The upstairs was simply a huge open room where men's groups met weekly on various nights. Ted Fulham and his parents lived between Grandma's and the store. Ted was a couple of years older, more the age of George and Danny than us other cousins, yet we all played together sometimes. We did some really stupid things, as all kids do in any era, such as throwing chinaberries at each other or, worse yet, shooting the berries with slingshots. It really was a wonder we didn't "put someone's eye out," as our parents warned.

One of our other games was to play with wood-
en guns that George's daddy (my Uncle Jack) had
made for us: After Jack cut the wood according
to our plans – an L-shaped piece with the short
edge, the gun "handle," at a pretty good angle – he
gave us all sandpaper and we sanded the corners
and smoothed the handle and barrel and then we
glued a snapping clothespin to the top edge of the
handle. We cut big rubber bands out of inner tubes.
These were our "bullets" and the width was important – too wide and it was too heavy to fly very far,
too skinny lessened control of the aim. One end of
the rubber circle looped around the tip of the barrel
and the other end was snapped into the clothespin.
Pinching the clothespin against the gun handle
released the band, sending it flying through the
air. They worked well, sometimes with surprising
accuracy.

And that's what almost got us into big-time trouble
one summer night.

Ruby didn't keep her store open at night, but some
evenings the place would liven up a bit. Cars would
arrive and line up beside and behind the store and
on the street. Men in suits and ties and hats filed
up the back steps to the meeting room. First ones
in would turn on lights, twisting each switch on the
sockets that held bare bulbs and hung from what
must have been a twelve-foot ceiling in that gigantic
second-floor room. From our vantage point across
the driveway and across the porch, the massive, col-
orless outside wall of the store began to glow with
shimmering golden rectangles. George, Ted, and I

would often lie there, belly-down on Grandma's side of Ted's porch, to spy on the mysterious men as they arrived and prepared for their secret meeting. One of those nights, with piles of ammo strips between us, we stretched our arms out onto the porch floor, steadying our weapons with our spare hands, and aimed up toward the open windows of the building.

In my mind, we might as well have been Roy Rogers and Gene Autry and Hopalong Cassidy – I would've been Hoppy, 'cause I liked his shirt and horse best. We waited patiently. When the men were seated around the room, there were more heads than usual visible to us through the upstairs windows, because this was a big meeting. We felt lucky that the first window in our sight had two heads showing; the second had one, and this gave us each a target in plain sight without having to move out and sacrifice our cover. Once the night was sufficiently dark and the men were still and quiet, we agreed on our assignments, tightened our aims and pulled our clothespin triggers, each of us hitting a man in the back of the head, much to our own surprise – and horror. Our attack stirred quite a commotion, and it was immediately evident that every man in the meeting was running for the door to come down and find us culprits! Of all the times we had done this, our rubber bands had only bounced off the side of the building, never even reaching the height of the windows, until now, when we all hit our targets at the same time, a good thirty-five feet away and twenty feet high. We grabbed all evidence – our stashes of guns and rubber band ammo – and hightailed it to the coal bin under Grandma's house.

We stayed hidden longer than the voices lasted as the men roamed around the homes looking for us, and we finally returned to our respective houses much dirtier than when we had left and in agreement that we would not tell our adult world – and that we would never do such a thing again.

Unlike Joe Williams, Ruby Furr was a humorless sort, to say the least, and from then on, any time I had to go into her store, I always thought she looked at me, not as Hoppy, but as the outlaw that I was.

~August 12, 2007~

Chapter 3

Command Central

It was crowded and hot and inconvenient in every imaginable way, so I'm pretty sure I didn't love Grandma's kitchen back then as much as I do now, from this distance of time. "Built-ins" were becoming the norm in newer homes, but there was nothing of the kind in Grandma's except for the sink, and being attached to the wall was its only redeeming feature. It was a wide, white basin, maybe thirty inches wide by eight inches deep, and it had its own backsplash. There was both a hot faucet and a cold faucet jutting out of that porcelain slab that climbed about twenty inches up the wall, and when hot water was needed, it was too hot because no one had yet conceived the notion of blending the two to come, more comfortably, out of one pipe. The worst thing about that damn sink was that it was so back-breakingly low that anybody accepting dishwashing duty had to bend nearly in half. I was already pretty tall when old enough to be trusted with the dishes – a bit of a mixed honor – and I can remember spreading my feet far apart so as to shorten myself instead of bending double.

The rest of the kitchen was filled with everything it took for Grandma to carry on her culinary operations. There was a tall four-door dish cabinet that sat between the sink and the sitting room door, but it wasn't big enough, so some things had to be sandwich-stacked on top of the refrigerator, around the radio that delivered Sunday morning sermons to her, and more dishes were stuck in any other cubby-holes that could be found. A white metal table with three shelves, just like in every other kitchen of the time, sat on the other side of the doorway, holding more dishes, cookbooks, and trinkets grandkids had bought or made for Grandma – if she considered them worth keeping.

I can't imagine there ever being an old gas stove that was used more than Grandma's. The temperature control in the oven never did work right, according to my memory, but Grandma knew exactly how to skirt around its shortcoming by cooking things a certain number of minutes longer than called for in the recipe. A lot of what went into that beast of an oven began life at the wood hutch in the other corner of the stove wall. God only knows how many coats of leaded enamel that thing wore over the years: a chipped spot revealed at least white, ivory, robin's egg blue, a darker ivory, white, yellow, and, the last I recall, a mint green that made it look like it had come from a hospital instead of Sears, Roe-buck. Whoever invented those hutches must have reincarnated to design RVs – there was no wasted space, and a lot of common sense went into the design. Come to think of it, they *were* called Hoosier Hutches, and most RVs are built in Indiana, so I just might be onto something there.

It sported a hinged bin on the upper left side that was lined with tin and into which fifty pounds of flour could be poured. At the bottom of the bin, conveniently over an opening where Grandma's bowl could be set to receive the beginnings of the best piecrust this side of the Atlantic, was a built-in sifter. Opened doors and drawers revealed other metal-lined sections that held her Morton's Salt and McCormick spices. There was Calumet Baking Powder as well as Arm & Hammer Baking Soda, her Softasilk Cake Flour and a bag of self-rising Gold Medal, sugar, Peter Pan Peanut Butter, Crisco, cornmeal, rice, dried peas and beans, measuring cups and spoons, and a gigantic tin of black pepper to satisfy my Aunt Toonsie's taste for hot. The hutch was always packed to the gills! Grandma must have baked every single day. She would decide what she wanted or needed to bake, head to the hutch, pull out the porcelain shelf that enlarged her work space, roll up the tambour door, grab the needed ingredients, and work her magic in Command Central. If she needed more space, she turned around and took over the kitchen table.

Ah, that kitchen table! What memories were made around it! The table was always covered with an oilcloth, usually blue checkered, that supported the Blue Willow plates we took turns overfilling with Grandma's good cooking. Along the backside of the table, under the window, there was a long bench instead of chairs. That's where we grandkids sat, unless of course there were enough adults to fill the entire table, and the rule "children should be seen and not heard" was engaged. In that case, we were hardly even seen, much less heard, as we were relegated to card tables in the sitting room and our mothers would bring our plates, filled with what they thought we should eat. Those choices weren't particularly based on the nutritional standards taught by the new USDA Food Pyramid. Not only did my family not know about the real facts of nutrition, they didn't know they should know. Just as my mama hadn't known it wasn't a good idea to fill my baby bottle with Coca-Cola or that it would begin an addiction to last me seventy-plus years. Sugar wasn't a treat, it was a standard, so cakes and pies and sweet tea were staples of every food occasion, and it's why some Southerners thought a Moon Pie and "a big R-uh-C" were a great meal.

Years later I left for East Carolina College to major in home economics – not because I especially loved cooking, sewing, and all the other things about home ec. In fact, I had been born a tomboy, and I couldn't imagine when entering ninth grade how I would fit into such a class; I tried my best to think of a way to get out of the requirement. I would have been much better in "shop," but we're talking 1956, and we had not come a long way, baby. No, I chose it as my college major not because I was a natural at the skills of homemaking, but for two other reasons. What I had loved about high school was my teacher, Lorine Kanoy Calloway. Having no clue what I wanted to do with any college degree, I learned from her that home ec was "a career with a thousand and one job titles," so I figured I'd find something that I'd like. How's that for life planning?

Actually, my college years did turn out to be fairly interesting, and I even discovered that I loved some of the subjects, especially textiles, designing, tailoring, and interior design, and the designing of house plans. A couple years after I had graduated and begun teaching in northeastern North Carolina, somebody in Birmingham launched *Southern Living*. The magazine eventually published hardback cookbooks – **The Bread Cookbook, The Casserole Cookbook, The Meat Cookbook,** and so on – one a year, and their recipes were chosen from entries sent in by home economists around the South. I had at least one recipe published in every cookbook, and I always gave my grandma a copy. She loved them. When she wasn't cooking from one, she was reading the recipes, reared back in her easy chair.

Meals at Grandma's were highlights of my weekend visits back home. She planned for my arrival and never once failed to have me over for a supper of her mouth-watering chicken livers. I didn't realize that what she was feeding me in the other meals was not something that had become standard fare during my absence, but I soon understood that she always picked things from one of "my" cookbooks to try out during my time with her. I would praise profusely the casserole we had just finished off, or the chicken dish, or the mashed potatoes that seemed just a wee bit more tasty than the usual, and I always asked for the recipe.

"Well, I got it out of *your* cookbook," Grandma would say, as if I should know every recipe, and then proceed to find the page, plus paper and pen for me. Invariably, by the time I copied all the ingredients and was well into the instructions, I would hear the caveat: "Now, I didn't use that much milk, and I used real onions instead of garlic salt. And I added just a little bit of lemon juice. ..."

I had copied a recipe to take home to my own version of Command Central, but it was for a dish I had not eaten.

~August 20, 2007~

Chapter 4

Concord Memories

During my childhood, Concord, North Carolina was a safe and comfortable little town. Union Street – the main one running north-south – had then, as now, a lining of giant oak trees whose arms spread to each other along the sides of the street as well as across it, shading the wide thoroughfare with a cool green canopy. Behind the trees on North Union, in particular, were the mansions that embraced the lives of the richest residents of Cabarrus County, among them Charles A. Cannon, the Cannon of Cannon Mills and the sheets and towels that many of us find covering our beds and bodies. That's not where my relatives lived. They lived in what might be called the "mill section" of town.

My mama grew up in a modest two-bedroom rental house at 187 Kerr Street, and my Grandma Helms and Aunt "Toonsie" lived together there until Grandma died in 1975. This was where my cousins Joanie and Ellen and I played house under the shelter of a mothering fig tree outside the sitting room window and lazed in the swing on the front porch on hot summer days, and it was where

I saw my Grandpa Helms lying in his casket in the living room when I was three years old. Toonsie was seventeen years older than I was and we were best friends for a long time. Sometimes we would take the bus and sometimes we would walk the thirty minutes to town from her house. When we walked, we passed by the school she had attended as a child. One day she stopped dead in her tracks and pointed at the school.

"See that window there on the corner of the second floor?"

"Yes."

"That's where I was in the second grade. See that window on the other corner?"

"Yep."

She laughed and said, "That's also where I was in the second grade." Then she told me about being really sick and missing nearly a whole year of school, having to repeat that grade.

My favorite trips to town were with Mama and Toonsie, and Porter's Drugs was the ultimate treat-stop. The black and white octagonal floor tiles and the shiny black counter and tables were a crisp and welcome sight as we chose which curly-wire-backed chairs we would sit on in the front part of the drugstore. The soda shop's tiny, round ebony tables offered adequate respite as we waited for our orders of the best egg or tuna or chicken salad sandwiches in town and their fountain Cokes, dark amber sweetness over finely crushed ice. The odd thing about the sandwiches was that before wrapping them in waxed paper and sending them to the tables, the cook "smashed" them by pressing them on the grill during toasting. On a really hot day we would forego the squashed sandwiches for a more refreshing sundae or banana split.

The drugstore was just off the square, where Union crossed Church, and a bit farther down Union Street were other stores that are seared into my memory. There was a jewelry store that, honest to God, was only about five feet wide. The jeweler was a Mr. Helms, though no kin to my family, and I remember how nice he was. We always stopped in just to say hello and enjoy his smile.

A few doors down from there was a great hardware store – even as a kid, I loved hardware stores! After my sister, Lori, was born and included in these Concord excursions, the four of us were walking down the sidewalk one day. I spotted a ladder set up in front of the hardware store. Nonchalantly, I climbed up one side of it and down the other. Lori might have been only four or so, but she wasn't too young to turn beet red with embarrassment. When I reminded her of this story recently, she said, "Well, you embarrassed me my whole life!" And it's true.

Then there was the F. W. Woolworth five-and-dime store where I had my first job when I was sixteen. I was assigned the candy counter as soon as I proved I could count and weigh without mistake, and I gained eight pounds my first week on the job. My boss told me I was eating up all his profits, and I told him I couldn't honestly recommend a product that I wasn't intimately familiar with. I worked there on weekends and during summers while in high school. Once when I was working at one of the large, central counters, I stood at the end straightening merchandise. I wore a dress I had made: buttoned to the waist in front, zipper in the back, and belted. I felt something fall down my back. I suppose I thought it was a harmless bug, and I stretched my arms out in front of me to tighten my dress on my back and kill the bug. Well, it wasn't a bug. It was a wasp. A really, really pissed off wasp! I went flying down to the basement where our break room was and one of the other clerks followed me. She opened up the back of my dress and found the wasp, which actually was dead by then, but not until after it had stung me twice and bitten me three times, too. I had no idea they could bite, but there were marks to prove it. Remembering something my daddy taught me, I sent someone to Porter's to get me a cigar and I chewed a bit of the tobacco and had my friend tape it to the stings with a Band-Aid to pull out the poison. I never reacted well to stings. I wasn't deadly allergic, but I was allergic – and I felt myself feeling hot and sick. I told my boss I had to go home. I'm not denying that chewing the tobacco might have been a factor.

I was a college freshman in the day of madras prints, wrap-around A-line skirts, and oxblood-colored Bass Weejun penny loafers. *Seventeen Magazine* selected "girls" to be magazine representatives, reporting about fashion events on campus and in our hometowns. I was one of those representatives

– which probably helped me land a summer job at a smart little clothing store, in fact called The Smart Shop, down near the end of the row of stores on that side of the street. I loved working there and buying clothes at discount.

But back to the earlier days...

My school days began with a choppy start in Sanford, North Carolina. A November birthday meant that I was a year "late" starting school, so I entered first grade at age seven rather than six like most kids. First grade wasn't half completed when my teacher called my parents in for a conference. She told them that, in her opinion, I should be moved up to second grade. Against my wishes and in spite of my tears, Mama and Daddy agreed with her, so I left friendships being newly shaped and a teacher I liked. I was moved into a new classroom, and being quiet and shy, I felt like an alien among students who had already formed their alliances for the year. Soon I realized everyone in the class was treated like they didn't belong there either. My three memories of the short time in that room consist of not wanting to go there, the teacher slapping everyone's open palm with a ruler (she didn't know who had misbehaved so she punished everybody), and being thrilled to death when I learned we were moving back to Concord and I wouldn't have to see that hateful woman one more day.

When Mama and Daddy and I moved back to Concord from Sanford, we lived in one of four roomy apartments that composed a square brick box on Kerr Street. The Folkmans lived there, too. Daddy had paired with Mr. Folkman to start the hosiery mill in Sanford. They came back to Concord when we did after the mill closed. The only other neighbor I remember there was an old man, well, older than my parents. I never saw him out of his easy chair, and I never saw him without a cigarette in his left hand. His fingers were as pointy as the nose on the front of his bald head, and the index and middle fingers on his cigarette hand were yellowed with nicotine. My only other memory there was one of torture. I had a lot of earaches as a kid, and the doctor would come to our apartment to "treat" me. Some treat! It took both Mama and Daddy to hold me down on the bed while the doctor "lanced my eardrum." That can't possibly be what he actually did, but that is what the procedure was called. And I screamed bloody murder. Every time.

Anyway, that's how I ended up living a dozen or so blocks away from Grandma's house, going to nearby Long Grammar School, and being in Miss Ila Bost's second grade class. After meeting her, I was disheartened it wasn't for the entire year. I wished I could do like Toonsie and repeat the second grade.

Ila Bost was the stereotypical "old maid school teacher" of 1950. Miss Ila, as she was called by students and parents alike, was appreciated for her expert teaching skills and joked about by many people for being just about the homeliest woman anybody would ever hope to see. Miss Ila couldn't help how she looked, and the jokes about her angered me, because I saw her differently: she was kindness personified, the person who was opening new worlds to me, and since all her inside goodness glowed way beyond her surface and filled the room and my life, I thought she was the most beautiful person I'd ever known.

There *was* one most unattractive woman in town, a woman I think of as "Miss JC" because I remember seeing her for the first time when Mama and I were crossing the street down by the courthouse on our way to JCPenney. As a child, she had a most unfortunate encounter with a horse that bit off her nose, leaving her with two cavities in the middle of her face where the bridge of her nose ought to be, and I was certain my eyes were being sucked right into those holes when I looked at her. That was creepy enough, having to face her, halfway through crossing the street, but I was mesmerized, and I kept on looking when we were directly beside her. Seeing someone who doesn't have a normal profile is a sight not to be forgotten. My brother-in-law says that we Southerners figure we can say anything we want to about anybody, so long as we preface it appropriately. For example, regarding Miss JC: "Bless her heart, she was ugly as sin, but she couldn't help it." If anyone ever reads this who knows my "Miss JC," I hope they will realize I'm not intending to be rude – it's just that her face really was a sight to behold.

My new and beloved teacher – such a contrast to the terror I'd left behind in Sanford – lived a few blocks still farther from the school where she had taught since God was born, for sure, and her home was in sight of my Grandma Helms's house.

Whenever at Grandma's, I would stare at Miss Ila's, longing to go visit although I never had the nerve. I could only imagine what that invisible, secret interior must be like: surely all the walls belonging to such a magical woman were lined with books and pictures, and there must be stories dripping from the corners, because Miss Ila knew everything there was to know and she helped me want to know it, too.

The next year we lived for a short while in a rented house on Carolyn Drive at the other end of town while ours was being built out in the country. I wished I could have known the people who lived there before us. Every interior wall had at least one archway cut through the baseboards so electric train tracks could run all over the house. Apparently that is what prompted Santa Claus to bring me a Lionel locomotive set that year. I still have it, and it still whistles and blows smoke. I think we had to finagle around some regulations, maybe claiming Grandma Helms's Kerr Street address as our own, but somehow I continued at Long Grammar School for the third grade. My best friend was the prettiest girl in the class, undoubtedly the prettiest in the school. For some reason, she was afraid of Miss McConnell – who was a good teacher but no Miss Ila. One day my friend needed to go to the bathroom but wouldn't raise her hand to ask permission. Soon, I saw a great puddle of pee on the floor around her desk and tears streaming down her face. Years later, during high school, she became my cousin's girlfriend, and whenever I saw her I always wondered: if that day had been seared in my memory, surely she remembered it, too. Of course, I never asked.

By the time I began fourth grade, I moved with Mama and Daddy into our new house on the farm where U.S. Highway 29 is intersected by Pitts School Road, about four miles south of Concord on the road to Charlotte. When Daddy was a boy – less than sixteen, but how much younger I don't know – he was riding in a wagon with his daddy, going into Concord to sell some of their farm-grown goods so they could buy flour and other staples they couldn't otherwise provide for themselves. He loved those trips with his daddy, and he especially looked forward to the stretch along Pitts School Road that took them past fields rich with corn and cotton and wheat, crops flourishing in the fertile blackjack soil that fed most of Cabarrus County. He pointed to a farm situated on the north side of the road and said to his daddy, "I want a farm just like that one when I grow up," aware of the difference between it and the scrappy land around their rental house, where they eked out the produce now in the back of their wagon. That was the very farm that Daddy bought when he got out of the Army and he and Mama had saved enough money.

My mother drew the plans for that farm house, looking at others in magazines and books and piecing together ideas to create one that she and Daddy thought would suit their needs and budget. It was a modest two-bedroom house, constructed before builders and planners, much less my mama, knew to include ample closets and electrical outlets and a bathroom big enough to turn around in, and not to use carcinogenic asbestos shingles as siding.

That's where I lived for the next nine years and on occasion for years thereafter during college breaks or for visits after I was "out on my own." Those years would always include regular visits into town – Concord – but the farm was Home, even when I didn't feel "at home" in the house or with my parents. Still, life on the farm created a new batch of memories, and I have yet to tell you about them.

~August 6, 2007~

Chapter 5

Mauldin's

"Afternoon, little misses." Bufe tipped his hat toward us just before lifting the two brown bags from the bed of the battered, black pickup with MAUL-DIN'S hand-lettered in arcs on the doors – emerald green letters with gold outlines – the four-digit telephone number in gold under the name. My cousins Joanie and Ellen and I were floating lazily in the porch swing when he arrived, and I ran to the back of the house to hold the screen door open for him. Grandma Helms waited in the kitchen as he lumbered, arms full of groceries, through the sweltering heat and up the four gray steps to the back porch.

In 1950, home delivery of groceries was not unusual. Although her children who lived in the area were happy to shop for her, it was a helpful service for Grandma who had no means of transportation and no interest in asking for help. She'd call the grocery store and give someone her order, naming the brands she preferred, of course.

"…and a quart of mayonnaise – now you be sure it's Duke's!" she'd say, and before long Bufe would pull up to the curb in front of her house to trade the groceries for some of the money that she kept in one of those old Duke's jars hidden in her kitchen. She also had a zippered coin purse that she had made, and when the groceries were somewhere between Barbrick and Kerr streets, she took the right amount of money out of the jar, put it in her little black bag, and slipped it into her apron pocket. Mr. Buford Torrence had been delivering her groceries for years and she knew he was trustworthy, but she didn't like for anybody to know where her grocery money stash was kept.

Mama and Daddy and I lived on a farm and we grew a lot of our food. Decades away from those days, I can still feel the memory of sitting under the young water oak by the back-door steps with Mama and Grandma Aldridge, all three of us in metal-frame folding chairs with bottoms and backs of woven nylon strips. Sticky with sweat and swatting bugs in that liquid summer heat, we shucked bushels of corn and strung buckets and buckets of green beans; we shucked peas and, worst of all, cut gooey, slimy okra. I learned early on that I had no intention of being a farm wife: canning and freezing was a lot of work, and Mama came home from a hard day at the mill only to spend her remaining hours until bedtime taking care of those necessary duties. Every night, she barely hit the sack before Daddy got home at eleven fifteen after finishing his second shift stint at the mill. Then she got up early enough the next morning to drive into town and be at her own machine in the same mill before seven o'clock. For a while in the summer, harvesting the garden got pretty hectic, and weekends were filled with little more than canning, freezing, and going to church.

In spite of all the vegetables we canned and froze and the beef we raised and kept in the freezer year-round, we still made plenty of trips to Mauldin's for staples – including our Duke's Mayonnaise! – and with every shopping visit my fondness for Bufe continued to grow. He not only delivered groceries to women like Grandma Helms, he was responsible for the produce section at Mauldin's Grocery. He kept all the fruits and vegetables neatly ordered, hand-sprayed with a mist, and he could answer any question about how to choose or how to cook or whose farm or what state had grown the food soon to be on your own table. Whenever Mama and I got to the store, I would always run ahead of her so I could have more time to say hello to my friend. And there he would be – with his spiffy white overall apron tied around his big waist, arranging his bins of fruits and vegetables, or collecting groceries for someone like my grandma. I knew that whenever he saw me, he would stop whatever he was in the middle of doing and visit with me. I had no idea how many children walked on those same darkly oiled wooden aisles that I skipped along; I didn't have to give them a thought, I had no doubt he looked forward to seeing only me. He beamed a smile whenever he saw me running toward him, knelt down in order to be at eye-level with me, and my eight-year-old heart was filled to the brim with love for that man.

On one of those Mauldin's days, Bufe was kneeling as usual, talking to me and to Mama, and I had what I thought was a great idea. Knowing Sunday dinner to be a special occasion at our house, and knowing Bufe to be a special person and that, in turn, so must his wife and children be, I turned and asked Mama if we could invite him and his family to come eat with us. My mother was stunned into silence.

Before she could speak, Bufe stood up, holding my hand and maintaining his beautiful smile. Saving my mama from her awkward embarrassment, this gentle and genteel black man spoke.

"That's very sweet of you, little miss, and I do thank you for the kind thought, but Sunday dinner is a very special time at my house, too, and my family likes to spend the time together."

I understood Bufe's reason for turning down my suggestion. What I didn't understand was Mama's explanation once we left the store: "Blacks and Whites aren't supposed to socialize."

~August 12, 2007~

Chapter 6

Beginning Life on the Farm

The farm was lying in wait for us when we moved
back to Concord in 1951. A slumbering giant of
eighty-five acres – small as farms might go, but huge
in Daddy's heart and mind – ready for his plans and
hard work and Mama's unending contributions. It
was Daddy's pride and joy.

We lived in town, but the three of us would go out to
the farm on Sunday afternoons, often with a picnic,
and we'd walk in the woods that Mama loved, trying
to avoid the irrepressible poison ivy. Daddy would
talk about what he hoped to do on the property,
and Mama imagined a picnic table in the beautiful
woods. In time, however, she gave up her wish for
the picnic table, and she stopped going to the woods
altogether: the poison ivy was too dangerous for
her. She once had such an allergic reaction to it that
she almost had to have her lower legs amputated.
Considering all the things I have already forgotten,
I wish the sight of her purple legs were one of them.
Her picnic retreat in the woods never happened, and
I have always felt that was the one thing she had
looked forward to in moving to the country.

Through time, the land that was ours had grown one decent-sized hill near the back north side, and a dirt lane went from Pitts School Road in front of our house on past that hill to the property behind. Daddy called it "the Weddington place," but it was "just land," he said, not a farm. Daddy firmly believed that land should be functional. Nearly fifty years later when I drove him and my stepmother out through my adopted Southwest that I had come to love, he stared out the window of the RV for a long time and then sighed.

"Why, this land ain't good for nothin' but to hold the earth together." That seems like enough to me but not to Daddy.

Mr. Stovall lived by himself on the far side of that property behind us. The Weddington family owned a lot of other land in the area, and I have a feeling that Mr. Stovall had been someone who had helped the older Weddingtons when they lived in that house; he might not have been far removed from a slave. He was obviously revered and, I suppose, was given a place to live after the old Weddingtons had died. He was a gentle, quiet, and slow-moving old fellow that my young mind figured to be about a hundred and ten. He lived down there, wedged between our farm and Coddle Creek, in a story-and-a-half house like most other hundred-year-old dwellings. Never painted, it was as gray as his curly hair and stubby whiskers, as weather-faded as his overalls. Although Mr. Stovall's eyes looked cloudy and had unintentionally worn into a mirror of much sadness, I always sensed a brightness about him.

I now wish I hadn't been so shy and would have talked to him more, learned something about who it was that lived behind that perpetual slight grin with its trickle of snuff spit trailing to the side.

Back on our side of the property line, a sweet, natural stream ran through the woods that stood in front of the hill, across a meadow. Daddy and I went down there often and sometimes Mr. Stovall would meet us by the stream. I was curious how he happened to know we were there: his house must have been a good tenth of a mile from that stream, down a weedy trail that led to his home. He and Daddy were always formal with each other – "Mr. Stovall," "Mr. Aldridge." He never called me anything but "Little Girl." Daddy kept an old beat-up, long-handled aluminum ladle hanging on a tree by the stream, and he instructed me how to drink from it if Mr. Stovall was with us. I was to avoid placing my lips on the ladle. Instead, I should place the edge of its cup below my lip and let the water slide into my mouth. Daddy had a thing about drinking after other people (and he instilled that in me) – any other people – but it was not lost on me that Mr. Stovall was Black and I knew that was a factor in Daddy's instruction. What amazed me most, knowing Daddy, was that he allowed the sharing at all. I liked that he did.

It was by that stream that I sat one day when Daddy was busy thinning brush. I sat on the bank, collecting little sticks, and I asked Daddy if I could borrow his pocketknife to whittle a bit. He gave me the knife and an admonition.

41

"Now, Monk, don't you drop my knife down one of those crawdad holes!"

The bank was riddled with them, and I doubted they were even big enough to swallow his knife. But one was.

Before we built our home, the only structure on our farm was another one of those old story-and-a-half houses. Unlike Mr. Stovall's, it was as dark and as aged as our ladle-buddy himself, but in much worse shape. In fact, the house had been built, apparently, around the time of the Civil War and must have been a pretty nice structure in its time. Its finery had long since faded and warped and sagged; some of the chalky bricks had fallen from the chimney top, and most of the bottle-glass windowpanes were broken or cracked. There were few boards left on the porch, so careful attention had to be paid when taking steps to the front door – or doorway, the door being long gone. The inside was strewn with some hay, strangely, and grass and leaves, the occasional dead squirrel and mice alive and dead, and an abundance of spider webs – and old whiskey bottles. But Daddy would always go in to check out the place when we made our trips out to the farm, and I imagine he was wondering about the people who had lived there. I don't know for sure if he wondered about such things, but my young mind did. And I wondered about the Indians who had lived there before them. I even wondered about the dinosaurs that must have made footprints in a distant time, and I wondered if the ocean had ever come in that far.

One Sunday afternoon we drove over the lane,

up the hill to park at the old house – it was steep enough that the car had to be put into second gear to drive to the top. Another car was already there. That day, Daddy told Mama and me to stay in the car while he went inside. Soon, a man and woman came flying out the door, nearly jumping across the snaggletooth porch, making the last adjustments to their clothes, with Daddy yelling at them never to come back or he'd have them arrested for trespassing. I suppose they had made good use of the hay. Eventually, Daddy tore down the rest of that relic, leaving only a part of the fireplace as a reminder of what once had held the lives of people we never knew, a family who must have loved the same farm Daddy fell in love with years later and that we kept for almost fifty more years.

Our own house was built in '52, according to plans that Mama had drawn to scale. She and Daddy pored over plans in magazines and books until they found one similar to what they wanted and could afford; they ordered the plans for that house and then altered it to their wishes. I can remember seeing her work on the drawings, meticulously calculating and measuring, transposing feet to quarter-inches on meat-wrapping paper. She learned from the blueprints they had ordered, and drew our house with the proper thickness of inside and outside walls, window placements, and door widths – two bedrooms, one bath, heating hall, living room, dining room, kitchen, large side porch, small back porch. Many years later when I worked for Virginia Electric & Power and helped homemakers with remodeling plans for kitchens and landscape lighting, I designed the new spaces and drew the plans with lighting and wiring layouts, and created storage areas according to items to be kept there, thinking how Mama would have loved to know back then what I had learned to do. I may have known how to draw more schematics, but I dare say I never drew any that were clearer or neater than hers. Going through some of Daddy's papers after he died in 2007, I found his records from building the house. It had cost five thousand dollars. A great sum for – and a greater tribute to the saving habits of – a man who never earned more than that amount in any one of his ninety-three years.

A few years after the house was built, Daddy had it veneered with brick. When it was five years old, Mama put her skills to work again, and Daddy hired a builder – and he and that one man built an addition of a large pine-paneled den with a grand marble fireplace and hearth, a utility room, and a double garage. Daddy asked Mama to design a half-closet under a bookcase to the left of the fireplace, a unit that had doors in the den and in the garage so he could place firewood in it without having to carry the dirty wood through the house. He was clever that way.

When I was about eleven or twelve, Daddy decided to farm more seriously while continuing to work in the mill. He would need help. His plan was to build a tenant house over on the hill, down the slope from where the old house once sat, and let a family live there in trade for working with him on the farm. It was a four-room house with a living room, two bedrooms, and a kitchen, a huge porch on the front and a small one on the back; it had electricity, but no running water – there was a well and an outhouse.

This time, I got to help, and my Daddy gave me one of the most important gifts of my life: he taught me carpentry. "Pride goeth before a fall" is not always true. I think I was never so proud as when I was on the roof of that house, nailing down the plywood sheathing! And I didn't fall off. I remember, too, the proud feeling of Daddy trusting me to do a good job. I remember his pride in telling people what a good helper I was. Daddy didn't have much of an education in terms of years in school, but he was quick with arithmetic, could figure out almost any problem, and could rig up the damnedest contraptions in order to carry out a solution that, physically, should have taken two or three people to accomplish. I doubt such things come with genes, but somehow I ended up like him in some of those ways. As I got older, he considered me to be more capable than he in such matters, and I could tell he had moved himself into the position of being my helper. Ironically, the last project we worked on was just before 2000 when we built sides for a trailer I had bought in order to bring things back to Tucson after cleaning out the attic of our house. The house would soon be torn down because we were selling the farm.

~August 31, 2008~

Chapter 7

Riddle Me This

I remember the first time I met someone who had never known her grandmothers. I felt sorry for her, as that admission made me notice what powerful forces my two had been in my life, and I felt most fortunate. Of all the adults I knew, they are the ones who impressed me in so many ways and provided me with abiding memories of growing-up-years spent in their company. Neither one of them had an easy life, and, beyond sharing relatives, that is about all they had in common.

Grandma Helms was a towering woman, five feet ten inches, over three hundred pounds, a strong, silent type.

Grandma Aldridge was of smaller stature and she hardly ever hushed even if she considered herself to be the only one within earshot.

Grandma Helms was a figure of authority.

Grandma Aldridge was emotionally needy and easy to have her feelings hurt.

Grandma Helms had a sense of humor but didn't like silliness; she had zero patience for rudeness of any kind.

Grandma Aldridge had a raunchy side.

I spent a lot of time with both of them, and anyone who knows me well can tell which traits I took from each one.

I was seventeen when my little sister was born, so I already had a lot of Grandma-years under my belt by the time she came along. By the time Lori was four or five – this little kid who was born with an envious sense of humor – she was helping me egg on Grandma Aldridge with some of her raciness.

The first time Grandma ever really shocked me was one day in the bathroom. I'm not sure how old I was, but I was getting ready for school and she came in to pee. She sat there a bit and then she said, "Did you know when you get older you go bald down there?

I said, "Oh, you do not!"

"Yes, you do!" she said, and she pulled her dress-tail up to show me. Not only had I never seen another woman's euphemistic "down there," I certainly had never imagined seeing one bald as a baby's butt, let alone my own grandma's!

Grandma Aldridge and I spent a lot of time washing dishes together when I was growing up, and I'm sure that chore brought up lots of memories of her own childhood. She had been an "illegitimate" child – a terribly unfortunate nomenclature for any human being. Her father was a married man of some importance, as I finally heard the story told, but – well, you know how those circumstances end, particularly in 1895. She never told me she "didn't have a daddy," but she did tell me about going with her mama to folks' houses and washing their dishes and that she carried a wooden box with her because she was too little to reach the wash basin without it. That's how they made a living.

If Grandma's bare-bottom boldness was immodest, the zenith of her raunchiness consisted of two riddles she taught me at our kitchen sink. The first one:

> *First white, then red,*
>
> *Stiff a-standin' in the bed;*
>
> *Not a lady in the land*
>
> *But what'll take it in her hand,*
>
> *Put it in the hole before,*
>
> *And wish she had a hundred more.*

Now, you and I both know what she's talking about, right? Wrong. I know, but I doubt you do. The second one (and remember, she called me "Carol"):

> *Under Carol's apron,*
>
> *A little round hole,*
>
> *Hairs all around it,*
>
> *Black as a crow;*
>
> *You can pull it and stretch it,*
>
> *Do it no harm,*
>
> *Put something in it big as your arm.*

Grandma with a one-track mind, you say? Wrong again. Actually, this does describe me as a young girl – only my "little round hole" was white, not black: it was a muff. And the first riddle? Think of "the

49

hole before" as a mouth. The answer? A strawberry. I asked her where she learned such things and she said her mama taught them to her. I'm guessing it was over somebody's dirty dishes, many decades before she taught them to me over our kitchen sink.

Being much younger and purer-of-mind than I am now, I was both mortified and thrilled to hear my Grandma tell me such naughty things. I knew they were our secret – until years later when we would initiate my little sister into our off-color club.

~April 26, 2008~

Chapter 8

Feline Love

One might say Grandma Aldridge was a prissy sort – she loved to dress up, she adored pink, and she liked for her hair to be a certain way. Few people knew her secret, raunchy side. I'll explain. But first, let me introduce her family.

When Halley's Comet flashed through the skies in 1910 – its first arrival in a hundred fifty-one years and its last appearance for another seventy-six – there was another arrival: the first of eight children born to Charles and Daisy Aldridge. Grandma was fifteen at the time. Four years later, my daddy came as the second. Grandpa died when Daddy was sixteen; his sister Lou was older, but consumption's claim promoted Daddy to male head of the family, a position that affected him, so far as I can tell, in lasting ways. Both sides of our family are filled with nicknames, and to this day, for me, there's an untrue sound when I hear Lou called Lula, Skeet called Nora, Nink called Lena, or Elt called Elsie. Somehow, Coy, Sam, and Charlie managed to keep the names on their birth certificates. Well, I'm sure Charlie is Charles, but that hardly counts as a bona fide nickname. Daddy, born Luther, was always called that by his own family, but to Mama's folks his name was Buddy or Bud.

Charlie was the youngest, and he lived with Grandma Aldridge in Kannapolis, North Carolina until he left for bible college in Los Angeles. And that brings up another matter: among Daddy's siblings, there was one actual preacher, Charlie, but there were others who might as well have been right there in the flock with him. Of the brothers, sisters, wives, husbands, nephews and nieces (my cousins), most were extremely active in the church, teaching Sunday school or Bible study, or singing in the choir and in special quartets or trios. My teen years fell within the heyday of "singing conventions" and "all-night sings." Coliseums filled with families like mine who sat for hours, listening and singing along with famous (if only in the South and among us) quartets who put the gospel message to music – the music that, along with that from the Black churches, spawned Elvis Presley and some of his backup singers. Lou's son, George Wayne, grew up to be a preacher, too, and I must admit, I considered it myself. I can get rather preachy at times, so a few years ago I ordered a minister's license online. Yes, you may call me Reverend. On Mama's side of the family – well, suffice it to say, that preacher-cup runneth over, even more.

The point is, Grandma Aldridge, along with her kids and grandkids, went to church "every time the doors were open" – Sunday morning Sunday school, Sunday morning preachin', Sunday evening choir practice, Sunday night preachin', Wednesday night prayer meetin', and every single night of the week if a revival was going on. I was one of those grand-kids, mind you, also attending Crusaders meetings. This was the youth group of the church, and we met every Sunday night at six before the regular service at seven.

Many members of both sides of my family attended the Concord Lighthouse of the International Church of the Foursquare Gospel – quite a mouthful, yes, but more commonly called "the Lighthouse" or, more simply, "church." Our church did not have a steeple: where a steeple should have been, there was a lighthouse – revolving light and all – right in the middle of town, in the Piedmont area of North Carolina. That light was a figurative and literal beacon to help any sinner come to the Lord. Even-tually, its beam directed me away.

The Foursquare denomination, settling its pros-elytizing somewhere between Southern Baptist and Pentecostal Holiness, did not "allow" drink-ing, cussing, gambling, not even PLAYING with cards, going to movies or plays (except at church, of course), dancing, wearing shorts, or fornicating outside of holy matrimony. Those things were con-sidered sins, and I soon surmised that 'most any-thing else that might be fun was probably a sin, too.

I tell you all of this so you will understand how strange it was to me that my grandma even knew – let alone absolutely loved – the word "pussy." Yes, *that* pussy. And it should come as no surprise that not one of her Bible-readin', God-fearin', church-goin', born-again children approved of her using it. Still, she *did* use it – in her own creative way – every chance she got with anyone who would tolerate it, and that was, by full count I'm sure, only Lori and me. Both of us offered fertile field for Grandma's racier side. She simply said "cat" every time she wanted to say "pussy." If her kids did happen to hear, they didn't scold her for this, they simply rolled their eyes and looked away.

It wasn't unusual for one of them to be near enough to overhear, because when Charlie left home in the late '40s, I think all of Grandma's kids decided that she should not live by herself any more. Instead of staying in her own home, surrounded by tangible significance and palpable proof of her life, she moved around from one child's house to the next, usually two to four weeks at a time, living out of her two suitcases. They weren't even new suitcases; they were handed down to her for this new existence, a situation I consider one of the saddest I've ever known since she was in decent health and, according to my best figuring, only fifty-one years old at the time they made her a gypsy. She was a part of each page of history known as the Twentieth Century except for its last five years and died when she was a hundred. Her final fifteen or so years confined my grandma to a nursing home bed.

That leaves what? Potentially thirty-five years to repack bags maybe every few weeks? However, when Nink or Elt or Lou or some daughter-in-law would have another baby, she'd stay a bit longer at that house, maybe for a couple months

54

to help out. There was one major exception. When my sister Lori was born, Grandma did not stay at our house for two months. She stayed about fifteen years. Daddy and I built a wall to close in the living room in order for her to have her own bedroom, but she still didn't have a closet. She had those two well-worn suitcases that she distrusted so much that she tied ropes around them, and she had her brown paper bag full of quilting scraps.

There's something curious about moving back home. By 1975, God only knows how many places I had lived, and I had called every one of them my home. But whenever I refer to the place where I lived with my parents, I also call that "home." "Home" with a capital H is more like it. The house, the address, the county, the state. It's all Home. Maybe it's a Southern thing, I don't know; whether or not, it must be as inbred as the accent is – natural, automated main-tenance of that sacred title, no matter how long and far away one has wandered from earlier physical roots.

When Mama died in February of that year, I had closed my business and was already living "at Home" with my white cat, JB, in order to be with Mama as much as possible during her nine months of final hospital days and to be with Daddy and Lori, who was just short of turning fifteen; I was thirty-two. Grandma Aldridge was there, too, and whenever we were both at the house, we had to share a bed. I was certain she was going to die in bed beside me. I would wake most nights and check her moonlit chest, praying for its tide, then go back to sleep, thinking, "Well, maybe not tonight. ..." Odd – at that time she was about eight years older than than I am now, but she seemed so old. Many mornings she would laugh, telling me I had talked in my sleep. Regardless of the pleading, she'd keep laughing and never once would tell me what I had said. Chances are, as a result, she knew me as well as I knew myself.

That spring, after Mama had died, Daddy got something that he said he had wanted all his life: a bloodhound. Before bringing Cammie home, Daddy wanted to build a house for this pony of a dog that had eyes like buckets and ears like saddlebags. He patched up a fenced-in space of ample dimensions for such a creature, and then I helped him with the house – and I mean HOUSE! Before the Alzheimer's set in, Daddy always seemed eaten up with common sense, so I have no idea why he didn't realize that the dog would have fared better during the bone-chilling dampness of those North Carolina winters in a smaller structure; but, no, this house was eight-by-eight at base, and six feet tall in the front, eight feet in the back. I've lived in apartments not much bigger. We installed a full, human-sized door. And a twelve-paned, double-hung window, for God's sake. Nevertheless, this was the doghouse, created mostly of bits and pieces of structural scraps lying around or swiped from other farm sheds and lean-tos that could spare a rib from here or there.

Whenever I was in the same vicinity as Grandma, she could hardly stand not being near me. I would frequently go to the bathroom with a good book, lock the door, and read until my butt was numb, just to have some peace and quiet. Still, I would hear her, plodding over the metal grid of the floor furnace outside the bathroom door, pretending to say only to herself with every circling, "Now, where DID Baby go? She was here a minute ago. ..."

Eventually, guilt unlocked the door.

More guilt was at play during the building of the doghouse. Daddy and I were spending so much time outside that I felt bad about Grandma being lonesome, so I went to the house and got her and a chair so she could be near us. She wasn't more than eighty years old by then, but she had already out-lived much of her eyesight and most of her hearing. Trying to communicate with her was a real pain; it took a lot of attention and energy, and that day I was quite tired and not wanting to have to yell. While Daddy went over the lane to the barn to get more wood, Grandma sat on her appointed throne against the back wall of the doghouse, and I lounged in the doorway. Thoughts ran their circles around my mind, incising ruts of guilt: *I know I should be talking to Grandma, but I don't feel like yelling; I know I should be talking to Grandma, but I don't have anything to say; I know I should be talking to Grandma, but I hate small talk; I know I should be talking to Grandma, but. ...*

While I kept the guilt growing and my mouth shut, I was looking at my hands and twiddling my thumbs. Then I noticed the two scars on one of my fingers. JB loved playing in brown grocery bags, and during playtime the night before I had not moved my hand fast enough when she bit through the paper. Aha! At last – something to say to Grandma, 'cause she loved to watch JB's antics in the bags!

I held up my finger and said, "Grandma, my cat bit me last night."

Without missing a beat, she said, "Well, keep your hands out o' your britches!"

I nearly fell off the doorsill, and when we both stopped laughing, she said, "Don't you *ever* tell anybody I said that!"

 I said, "Grandma, I promise you, I'm going to tell everybody I can!" And I have.

~August 4, 2007~

Chapter 9

What Goes 'Round...

Sometime around 1985, a habit was born. Truth be told, I've maintained less healthy ones with a lot more vigor and devotion; I've let this one slide from time to time, but lately, on occasion, I've resurrected its loveliness.

At the time, I was living in a garage apartment in Bowling Green, Ohio that felt like living in a tree house, especially every summer when the house became infested with little beetles of some sort from the elder tree outside the bedroom window. One night I was propped up in bed with a stack of magazines that a friend had passed down to me months before: Antiques and Architectural Digest. Hardly my usual fare, but thumbing through one, I came across an article written by a woman in Laramie, Wyoming.

 She told of driving to some place in the northern Georgia mountains to visit her grandmother whom she hadn't seen for many years, and arriving to find that her grandma and a slew of friends filled their time, quite happily, making quilts. They created quilt after quilt, talking about everything under their Georgia sun, laughing with and at each other, eating, and taking turns keeping each finished quilt. The granddaughter was quite moved by what she saw and what she felt among this group of older women, and was further touched by their acceptance of her, this younger visitor taken into their fold, into their quilting circle. She was there in time to enjoy and share their thrill at finishing a quilt they had started a few months before. She told how being a part of that, of them, became a part of her. Maybe she didn't really say that, but that's what her experience told me.

Time came to return to Laramie and she sadly packed her things while her grandmother and her friends made and packed food for her long trip 'cross country. A couple of the women, all of whom had gathered at her grandmother's to see her off, carried her bags to the car so her time could be spent in last minute familial savories.

They put convenient nibbles in the front seat beside her, placed her meager overnight needs in a small case in the back seat, and her other luggage in the trunk. She drove away, tears mixed with the memories, the feelings, of hearts full of laughter and love and creativity.

She arrived home and opened the trunk of her car to find that the women had hidden the finished quilt under her suitcase. She cried.

And so did I.

This woman's story had reconnected me with my

own Grandma, who had spent more hours than can be counted making yo-yo quilts. Even when she could barely see, she did it "by feel." I would take about twenty-five of her needles, thread them for her with four feet of thread knotted on one end, stick each one into a small piece of paper, roll the paper around the needle for safety, wrap the thread around each one, and put her new stash of tools into a Ziploc bag. She could then pull a five-inch circle of fabric from the bagful that my aunt had cut for her, take out a needle, run the basting stitch around the circumference, and pull the thread tight to make the "yo-yo." Once she had made a few hundred of them, she would sew them together, side by side, to make a quilt – or more usually, a coverlet.

How it made me wish I had one of her quilts...

I looked at the clock: 11 p.m. Laramie: 8 p.m. I picked up the phone and called information. I gave the operator the writer's name – a name I wish I could now remember. She gave me a number. I called.

A woman answered the phone.

"Are you _____?"

"Yes," she answered tentatively.

"Are you the _____ who wrote an article about your grandmother and quilts?"

"Yes."

I told her how moved I was by her story and what

it had meant to me. She said she had gotten a lot of response to the article soon after its publication – about eighteen months before – but no one had mentioned it in a long time. She said, "You have no idea how much I needed to hear this today. You have made my day!" We talked, we laughed, we shared Grandma-stories, and she said if I ever came through Laramie, call – she'd make tea. I didn't make it to Laramie before I forgot her name, or I would've called.

I would have called, and over that cup of tea I would have told her how she helped me form a new habit. I kept thinking about "You have no idea how much I needed to hear this today" and I determined then and there that whenever I read, hear, or see art that touches my spirit – something that another human being has honored enough to allow it to come through them and put out into the world – I will do whatever it takes to thank them, to tell them that my life is richer because of their efforts. Because of their surrender to the muse, because of their honesty, because of their generosity, a web is woven that connects one spirit to another to another to another, just like Grandma's yo-yos.

~August 29, 2008~

Chapter 10

Willow, Weep for Me

A perfectly round hole was bored in the roof over-hang of the backyard pump house, not three inches above where my hand would have to be, and it always made me uneasy. It was just above the spigot that had to be turned on to wash the car or to give the pot of flowers by the clothesline a drink of water or to clean off the top of the stump where Grandma had taken the hatchet to the old rooster's neck in preparation for a supper of chicken and dumplings. I never knew if the giant black and yellow bee was going to be at home when someone yelled, "Go turn on the hosepipe!" I would weave my way through the hanging branches of the weeping willow, trek through the tall, summer grass, watching for a snake, never seeing any sign of one, of course, but mainly looking for any thought that might keep my mind off the bee.

Many years later, when I lived with Ellen out in the sandy boonies of eastern North Carolina, our well was in the front yard, not the back, and it was pro-tected from the elements by a small plywood struc-ture that could be tilted up and back out of the way if any work had to be done on the pump. As scraps

were being tossed aside by the men applying aluminum siding to her old family home we were living in,
she asked if they would use some of them to veneer
the weathered old plywood pump house. By the time
they finished the sparkly white walls and we added
fresh black shingles to its roof, everyone wanted to
know why we had put our doghouse in the front yard.
And it did look for all the world like one. So much
so, in fact, that I took my sign paint and brushes out
one day and painted a big, black faux-doorway on
the road-side of the little building and lettered the
name of the "dog" over the arched top: PUMP.

That pump house I grew up with, though, was
lots bigger. It had a real door – one tall enough to
allow us, with a bit of a stoop, to go inside – and
Daddy had rigged the roof so that it could be tilted
up – although it was heavy as all get-out – to allow
adequate headroom and light if the pump had to be
worked on. Its sturdy pine skeleton was hidden by
a veneer of brick, except for the overhang that was
home for that bee. No matter my expected viciousness of a flying critter, Daddy would always tell me,
"Don't worry, Monk – they won't sting this month."
That man could go 'round his elbow to keep from
telling a lie, even if, in essence, that was exactly what
he was doing. Like what he told me about those
giant, Ice Age boulders over by Jackson Training
School in Concord. He said that they turned over
every time they heard a train whistle. I believed anything my daddy told me, and after years of my buying his assurance that I was not going to be stung, he
admitted that it was the *month* that the bee wouldn't
sting – but it could have stung me. Oh, brother!

Opposite the spigot side of the well house was the tall, skinny gas tank. Daddy had the five-hundred-gallon tank buried and the pump installed soon after we moved to the farm, and that's how we filled the car, the pickup, tractor, and lawnmowers. On a farm such an instrument was a necessity, but it seemed more a "specialty" to me, because not a one of my school friends could go into their back yard and put a gas nozzle in their family car. In that respect, the old thing wasn't too much unlike tanks today, but follow that hose back to its tank, and the picture is very different.

It was about eight feet tall, I reckon, and its silver -painted bottom was just slightly cone-shaped; there was a small door on the side that, when opened, revealed a gauge that told how much gas was still in the underground tank. Above the base was a clear glass cylinder with a centered vertical rod that had small metal plates attached to it, with numbers printed on the plates, reading one to ten from bottom to top. Back and forth, back and forth, we would pump the long black lever on the side of the silver tank – much as one pulls at a slot machine – and amber-colored gasoline would eventually begin to show, rising into the glass container at the top. It didn't take much pumping to wet a rag when we needed to "wash" ourselves down with gasoline in order to kill chiggers after picking blackberries over by the barn, and we might manage to wriggle the lever enough even without unlocking the heavy log chain that prevented anyone else from having their way with the lever and our precious gas. But if we needed to put ten gallons in the car? Well, it took a lot of pumping to lift that much gas out of the ground, and it was all that could be pumped into the reservoir at one time. Once the goal was met, the black rubber hose was removed, and the nozzle was placed in the car tank. As the car was fed, the gas level lowered behind the tank's glass window: nine gallons left, eight gallons, seven…until the fill had been administered. No electricity to help the process – gravity did the work.

This was an old Cities Service tank, and the top had white ad-glass that said so: two round pieces, one showing toward the front and one toward the back. "Cities Service" arced at the top (today it would read "Citgo"), with the logo in the middle and the word "GAS" at the bottom. In years to come, it was that bottom word that provoked me to hang one salvaged side of the antique glass in my bathroom. In some move to somewhere, it was broken, and there were probably a lot of people more pleased about that than I was.

In the days of my childhood and for some years beyond, it was permissible to burn trash outdoors. There was no such thing as recycling – except the kind that Daddy did for himself by never throwing anything away (of course, that didn't necessarily mean he would ever reuse the stuff!) – and there was no such thing as trash pick-up in the country. A fifty-gallon barrel always sat behind the pump house, and that's where we burned all our trash, always standing close by the stinking thing with a poker-stick, watching for sparks and any flying, burning scraps of paper. After all, there was grass, there were cotton fields and sheds, and there was a gas tank just a few feet away.

Those three sides of the pump house were home for vital parts of our life on the farm, not to mention that fat carpenter bee's, but the front side was the most important to me: towering by the pump house's door was the most beautiful weeping willow I have ever seen.

Climbing trees had been a favorite pastime for me since I first discovered that life offered that possibility, and that tree was perfect for climbing. The limbs started low, and, for certain, they had arranged themselves perfectly for me, so I could easily almost walk up into the tree, then actually lie inside its swaying arms. Possibly fifty feet away and across the driveway that circled behind the house was the back door to where Mama and Daddy and I lived, but I never felt "at home" there – in the house or, sad to say, even with my parents. As silly as it may sound, I felt then – and still do, mind you – that that sweet old willow loved me just as much as I loved it, and its heart was my home. Nobody beat me; in fact, I had only one spanking in my life, one from Daddy and a threatened one from Grandma Helms. Nobody starved me; we always had plenty of food and ate a lot. Nobody locked me in some closet; God knows we wouldn't have had one to spare. So it wasn't that I was really mistreated, I just never felt I belonged there.

Where I felt I did belong was in that weeping willow. Whether happy or sad, hiding in the tree was where I wanted to be. Sometimes I did hide behind its summer thickness: Mama would come to the back door and call for me – probably to clean my room or carry out the trash or just to come inside – and I would pretend I didn't hear her. Through its branches, I stared at the sky, out past the clouds, and felt that "out there" somewhere was my real home, and sitting in my tree was as close as I could come to being there. I watched the clouds as they accumulated during late afternoons and saw them turn into dogs and turtles and airplanes and pop-corn way up there in my "sky yard." In the safety of that tree was where I wrestled with The Great Questions: Who am I? Why am I here? What is my purpose? What am I supposed to do? Is there a god? I imagined. I dreamed. About what, exactly, I don't remember, but I smiled a lot. Perhaps I cried there even more. Not only did I not hear answers to my questions, I also climbed far enough into the tree to reach puberty where there was a lot to cry about, even if the tears could not be named. I talked to God, just in case there was one.

The willow was my haven.

After I graduated from college and was living and teaching three hundred miles away, I drove back to the farm to visit my parents and little sister on the farm. I pulled into the driveway to park back by the pump house. There, where my precious friend had swayed, had sung, had nurtured me, had rocked me to heaven and back, stood only the stump of my tree that Daddy had cut down while I was away.

~August 24, 2007~

Chapter 11

Gender-ly Speaking

Generally speaking, girls growing up today are aware of having more options than those of my generation had, although they are likely to take that for granted. In 1951, when my school first formed a band, I was in Miss Watson's fourth grade at Harrisburg School. My parents and I talked it over, and, yes, I could "go out" for band. I wanted to play trombone. During the first meeting of interested students, the band director instantly cut my water to a drip: "No! Girls do not play trombones."

"Well," I said, "I'll play a saxophone."

"Girls don't play saxophones."

"I'll play a trumpet."

"Girls don't play trumpets."

"Cornet."

"Girls don't play cornets."

"What *do* girls play?"

"Clarinets and flutes."

I chose the clarinet by default, a default determined by someone else, by gender bias, not by me.

There was something about the trombone that spoke of flexibility and surrender: the slide was an extension of the arm and a sort of visible breath, easing sound in and out, allowing the music that came from that Mysterious Place, through the player, and into the world. Those other instruments, down the list from my preference, seemed just that: more of an instrument than a partner. Keys pressed, holes covered, these had to be told what to do, commandments rather than cooperation. That's what it looked like to me anyway, and I wanted to be a part of what appeared to be a more natural flow of sound becoming music.

During the nine years I was in the band, our troop of musicians swelled to a respectable size for such a small country school, and we were mighty proud of ourselves in our handsome black and gold uniforms, strutting our stuff in parades. I don't remember how many members made up that little band the first year, though, only that there were very few of us. So few, in fact, that we didn't have enough to march in the Christmas Parade like other normal school bands: we rode packed in the back of a pickup truck! Our little Christmas Combo, blowing out numbers like "Jingle Bells" and "Rock of Ages," of all things.

It was the South, after all. And my first awareness that life was not always fair to girls.

~January 19, 2015~

Chapter 12

Win-Win

Wasn't always easy being a tomboy.

It was a perfectly natural state, mind you, and it was a state that came in mighty handy living on a farm. I always felt like Mama ought to celebrate the fact instead of spending so much energy trying to turn me into someone I wasn't, trying to make me look like somebody other than myself.

Even when I was too young to wash my own hair, while it still coiled down my back in platinum blonde slinkies all the way to my butt, she would have me climb onto the kitchen cabinet. I'd lay my long, lean self out across the cracking, red vinyl counter top, uncomfortably arching my back over the edge of the wide, porcelain drain board, and allow my locks to dangle into the sink. When Mama died, everybody called her a saint, but any time I remember her washing my hair, I have serious doubts. I assure you there was nothing saintly about her when she combed or brushed my hair.

All I ever wanted to wear were jeans and Mama tried her best to dress me in frills and lace and patent leather shoes – and new duds on Easter Sunday. The only passion I knew surrounding Easter was my hatred for the day.

I must have been about nine when Mama and Daddy began to let me sit a few rows behind them at church so I could be with my cousins – but we were given strict rules for our behavior.

One particular Sunday night two things happened: one surprised Mama, the other mortified her. She didn't know it, but after our usual spat about what I was expected to wear to church, and after she won, I went into my room to get dressed. "Win-Win" had not become the positive phrase it is today, but my young mind did believe in fairness, and I saw no reason why we shouldn't both have our way: I put on my fancy dress, and then I put on my jeans – and rolled them to above my knees. Totally undetectable!

I needed the jeans on that night, you see, because they had pockets. I loved marbles almost as much as jeans, and my mama, six rows in front of me, figured out my entire scheme when everyone in the church heard a fistful of marbles hit the hardwood floor, rolling their way slowly past my mama's feet.

~March 7, 2009~

Chapter 13

To and From

I grew up in a family of church-goers. We went to church a lot. The Foursquare denomination to which we belonged spewed its brimstone doctrine with vigor, settling its proselytizing somewhere between Southern Baptist and Pentecostal Holiness.

The family became loaded with preachers – uncles, aunts (yes, women pastors, but mostly pastors' wives), and several cousins went away to bible college and returned as ministers. One of those cousins was asked to come to hold a revival in a small church in Salisbury, North Carolina. About three nights into the week, he had finished his sermon and had delivered the requisite "altar call," that invitation to walk down to the front of the church and be prayed with, an expression of "giving one's life to Jesus, one's personal savior." He later told me that as he looked out over that little sea of faces one face in particular drew his attention. It was the face of a little girl who was staring at him; he said he recognized that look and knew she wanted to be like him – because, he said, he had the same experience when he was her age. He said he realized everything he had been telling these people was a lie.

Courageous in his conviction, my cousin turned to the pastor of the church and said, "If you want this finished, you have to finish it – I'm out of here."

He walked out and never looked back.

~March 7, 2009~

Chapter 14

Innocence Lost

In 1949, Sanford, North Carolina probably had a population of no more than five thousand people, and that year my mama, daddy, and I added three to the census. We moved there when I was six because Daddy had sunk everything he had into starting a full-fashioned hosiery mill with a co-worker of some years at Hugh Grey Hosiery in Concord, North Carolina, Mr. R. A. Folkman, a square-jawed bespectacled man of generous stature and closely held means. In nearly no time, full-fashioned went "out of style" and we went out of Sanford after only barely more than a year. But before we left, my young life accumulated experiences that burned into my memory during the time that spanned my sixth and seventh years, some to be repressed for ten years. I can't remember going to Sanford; I only remember being there – and all that I lost, along with Daddy and Mr. Folkman losing the mill.

Don't get me wrong, it wasn't all bad. Sanford was a small town in the late '40s, and I've always remembered it as bucolic. The farm fields that surrounded it crept into its edges, and the stately trees and lush lawns continued the feel of country all the way to the main street. Actually, there were some good things about that short time in Sanford. Five things, the best I can figure: it's where I learned to read; it's where I started school; it's where I had my first school chum, Judy Glass who lived on Green Street; it's the only place I can well remember living where we had neighbors we knew and loved, the Blalocks; and I had my beloved Lassie, who was my very best friend and protector.

We lived in two places during our short time there. The first was an apartment, a second-story apartment that had a tiny back porch at the head of long, steep stairs. In the winter, icy steps scared the bejeezus out of me. We didn't know very many people yet when November rolled around, really just mill associates and their families and our next-door neighbors, but my mother wanted to give me a birthday party and invite a few of them over. She made my favorite cake at the time – chocolate with white buttercream icing – and set it in the center of the kitchen table in its place of honor. We went downstairs to greet the guests, and when we brought them upstairs, my birthday cake had *red* icing: I never understood how those damn ants found it so fast – being winter, being upstairs – but my cake was mortally covered with tiny red ants! I can still see Mama dumping it into the garbage can. It's the first gut-wrenching disappointment I remember. Little did I know it was an omen.

I was still six years old when we made this life change, and how I remember much of my freedom there was in the hours on end spent with Lassie. She was a beautiful collie with a long nose and silky hair that I brushed every day. I think of her every time I see Barry Manilow. Every day we went for a walk. Highway 421 ran right through town as the main street, and we lived just two houses away from it. Lassie and I would walk up the hill to the corner, turn, go down about half a block, climb up on a cement wall that ran along the front yards of all the big houses there, and watch the traffic go by. I would look at the people in the cars and trucks and wonder where they had come from, where they were going, what they would do when they got there. I would read license plates, enjoying the special wonder of seeing a rare one from outside North Carolina. Already I loved numbers and would add the digits as quickly as I could. I would pump my arm when a semi drove by, and when the driver would pull the cord for his air horn, I'd laugh and Lassie would bark. On all our walks, she always placed herself between the street and me. No one ever taught her to do that. She was my pillow during afternoon naps. She was the beat of my heart.

In the late afternoons, Mama would fix what amounted to a picnic, and she and Lassie and I would go to the mill so we could have supper with Daddy. This ritual took place for months, I guess, until finally the day after one of our picnic-suppers, I woke up to find Lassie sick. When I got to her, she was lying on our small porch, on her side, and the skin on her stomach was almost transparent and greenish. Unbeknownst to us, as cool weather had come, mice had infested the mill, and Daddy had placed rat poison throughout the building – on crackers. It was Lassie's last picnic. It was my first broken heart.

Soon after that, we moved into a large house next door to this apartment. I'm not sure it was as huge as I remember it being, perhaps it seemed so compared to the upstairs we had shared with the ants. I'm sure the absence of my best friend made it larger and emptier. The thing I am sure about, however, is that it was the filthiest place I have ever seen. The kitchen had caked-on grease everywhere – even around the floor molding and under the cabinet toe space. While Daddy was at work, Mama and I sat on the floor with putty knives and scraped rolls of old, dried, greasy dirt; then we scoured everything with Spic and Span, and painted. It was the kind of dirt that you taste for years when you try to swallow the memory.

Eventually, it became a good place to live for two reasons that I recall. It is where I would lie in bed at night and Mama would read to me, until one night I surprised her by telling her I wanted to read the book to her. The other reason is that the Blalocks were our neighbors. They were my "old folks," which probably meant they were in their forties, maybe fifties. They did seem like grandparents to me, showering me with love and presents. And oh! Mrs. Blalock is the only person I have ever known who could actually make Moravian spice cookies! If you haven't had Moravian cookies, you have not lived. The recipe goes back to the seventeen hundreds in old Moravia, they have all sorts of spices and molasses, they are rolled paper thin, are known as the world's thinnest cookie, and I can eat them till my mouth hurts. Of course, she made me feel she made them just for me.

As much as I loved Mr. and Mrs. Blalock, and Mrs. Blalock's Moravian cookies, I even more loved their daughter, Molly. Molly was their only child, just as I was my parents' back then. Molly was in her mid twenties, had graduated from college, was really smart, athletic, beautiful, and she was my first crush. I couldn't wait to see her every day, but fell mute around her until she made me feel at ease. We became great buddies. Then Molly got married. I was crestfallen that she was going to move away, but I would have taken that happily instead of what really happened. Molly's husband was a pilot and had his own plane. They had flown in to see her parents and were headed back to where they lived in Pennsylvania when their little plane disintegrated in midair. In my sleep, I would dream of her beautiful face, her smiling at me. Perhaps she really was.

The state required a student to be seven years old when classes began in August and I wouldn't be seven until November of '49; that meant I had to wait until August of 1950 to enter first grade. So when I finally enrolled, it was only three months before my eighth birthday, and I felt completely out of sync: I didn't want to go; I was shy; I was tall for my age; I was "old." Once there, I loved my teacher and I loved learning. I loved going home every day and telling Mama what I had learned, and she would watch me do my homework while Daddy was spending all sorts of hours at the mill. Soon, I made a friend, Judy Glass. I never saw her after Sanford, but for over six decades her full name in my memory has been "Judy Glass who lived on Green Street." We lived fairly close and we were able to walk to school together. Thank goodness, because we were not to be classmates for long.

After I was in first grade for about six weeks, my teacher called my parents in and told them that she wanted to move me up to second grade. When they passed the news to me, my tears poured. I had barely adjusted to school at all and had come to love my class; now I had to move into a whole set of new people, a new teacher. And that new teacher was a hellion. Downright mean. One day someone threw a spit-wad but no one confessed. She made all of us stand by our desks, hold out our left hand, palm up, force our fingers down with our right hand to tighten the palm, and she came around with a wooden ruler and whacked every one of us on the hand. Hard. I came close to hating the woman. The year couldn't end fast enough. Fortunately for me, we left town after a couple months in her class and I finished the second grade back in Concord.

1950 was safe and peaceful compared to these days, and Mama was agreeable to my playing outside so long as she knew where I was. She told me never to go anywhere without letting her know first and I always honored that rule. I didn't like to be in-side, so Lassie and I would go on our outings or, after she died, I would ride my Red Flyer Scooter up and down Summit Drive. I was a whiz on that scooter! Our block of Summit Drive was short and on a slight hill. There were two houses between ours and the highway at the high end of the street, and the Blalocks' house and the gigantic First Baptist Church were on the low side where Summit butted into Steele Street. The church sat high on a hill, and I remember thinking that somebody would really want to go to church to climb all those steps to that front door.

One afternoon I was riding up and down the sidewalk and as I rode by the church toward the corner I noticed a truck on Steele Street. I thought it was stopped for the traffic light, but as I got closer, I realized it was parked there, and the man driving it was calling to me.

"Little girl, come here!"

I slowed my scooter. "What?"

"Come over here. I've got something I want to show you.

I walked the scooter toward the truck.

"Get up on the running board. I want to show you something."

I parked my scooter and stood on the running board. I saw what he wanted to show me. I had never before seen a penis, I had never before seen semen, and I'd never seen either or both all over a steering wheel and a man's pants between his knees.

Then he said, "Come go for a ride with me."

Dutiful daughter that I was, I said, "I'll have to go ask my mother." And I ran – beside my scooter, not on it – back up the hill to the house.

I knew something was wrong but I had no notion of the danger that had been so close. All I remember of what followed is Mama calling Daddy at the mill, his rushing into the house, Mama crying, and the police coming to the house and questioning me. It's a wonder I didn't notice his license plate; I loved numbers and was paying attention to the makes of cars and tags back then, adding the numbers on the plates. I guess I didn't want to look back as I heard him drive away. I did describe the truck to the policemen: dark green, dusty, a lumber truck, no lettering on the doors, flat bed, old two-by-fours standing upright along the side, grayish wood. And I described the man, his khaki pants and shirt – and the rest of his trimmings. They never caught him. I don't know if they ever even looked for him.

Neither do I remember anything else about Sanford after that. I think that Mama went into hysterics and that I was traumatized by her response and probably Daddy's, too, more than by what I had actually seen. I have no idea what I might have heard Mama and Daddy say about it, but I completely suppressed the memory until it resurfaced years later when I was a freshman in college. A friend and I had gotten temporarily locked out of the dorm and inside the fenced courtyard in our attempt to go down the back way to the canteen. We barely managed to get back in the dorm before the last door was locked and we then went through the dorm halls to reach the canteen; when we got to that first floor corner of the dorm, we saw that all hell had broken loose. Apparently, just as we were leaving the courtyard, a man had scaled the fence, stood outside a window where two beautiful coeds lived, and proceeded to smear his semen all over their window screen. As soon as I saw that screen – and realized how close we had been to him – the Sanford experience came back in a flash.

Not long after the near kidnapping, the mill closed. We packed all our belongings and moved back to Concord. But I had left a lot in Sanford.

~June 12, 2008~

Chapter 15

It's All In a Name?

I had never been around a baby – that is, my arms had never been around one. I was a senior in high school, it was April 4, 1960 and on that day I ceased being an only child: my mama had a baby.

She and Daddy had given me the honor of naming my new little sister, and I had done that well before she joined us. What no one knew was that I named her after two brothers that I was dating – Larry and Dennis – and my fresh, little sibling-to-be became Lori Denise Aldridge, even before she was born.

And then she came home. I stood over her crib, looked at her, this tiny new life, so, so tiny, and she looked at me, and – believe this – we both laughed. I swear, the child was born with a sense of humor! I stood there staring, afraid to pick her up, and said, "Well, isn't she a cute little rat!"

From then on, that was my nickname for Lori. Mine and mine alone – she did not allow anyone else to call her "Rat." Well, who could blame her?

My parents lived in a smaller world than the one

that I hoped for Lori, and whenever I returned home from college on weekends and during summers, I made sure to take her to out-of-town restaurants so she could experience ethnic food – experience anything rather than being stuck on the farm. She was about five when I took her to her first Chinese restaurant in Charlotte. As we stood in the lobby waiting to be seated, I noticed the Chinese calendar on the wall and explained to Lori what it was. She asked, "What am I?"

Lori was the Rat.

~March 7, 2009~

Chapter 16

Saint Luther

Back in the fourth century in Armenia, there was a Saint Blaise, Bishop of Sebaste. Anyone who had a throat disease summoned his help because he had once cured a boy who had swallowed a fish bone. On his saint's day, February 3, the Benediction of the Throat is a ceremony that is still carried out in London at St. Ethelreda's Church. I believe that there should also be a St. Luther's day, in honor of my daddy.

Daddy was a strong man, he was smart, he was cour-ageous, but he was also fearful in many ways. Well, at least fearful enough to exercise great caution about many things – and to teach me to do the same.

My family gathered often at my Grandma Helms's house for meals, and frequently, especially after our fishing trips, we had scrumptious fish fries. Those fishing excursions usually wielded crappies, fresh-water fish about the size of a small hand. And a little fish has lots of little bones. My daddy taught me from an early age to be extra careful eating fish, to make sure I removed all the bones before taking a bite, or else a bone could get caught in my throat.

Now, mind you, I never knew any people who had fish bones get lodged while swallowing, nor had Daddy. But it was possible and something to be feared.

You know where I'm going with this, don't you? I was about six years old at the time, we were chowing down on our Friday night batch of fish at Grandma's – and I felt myself swallow a bone! I must've looked terrified as I announced what had happened. After all, Daddy had instilled the fear of Neptune in me! But Daddy? He remained totally calm, got up from his chair, and pulled mine out from the table.

"Come on, Monk, let's go to the bathroom. All you have to do is pee. ..."

We did, and I did. When I finished peeing, I stood up and looked in the toilet: there floated one single fish bone. Such relief! I was safe!

I have always wondered if Daddy did some really fast thinking that night, or if he had always planned what he would do were I to swallow a bone: as we left the table, he brought a bone from his plate with us to the bathroom, and as I stood from the toilet, he simply dropped it into the water.

~January 19, 2015~

Chapter 17

A Full-Fashioned Race Track

On Highway 29 between Concord and Charlotte and about five miles south of our farm lies a tract of land that had been a working plantation during the Civil War. In 1959 earthmovers were unleashed on that hill, and the property is now known as Charlotte Motor Speedway.

The major race event in its early years was The World 600, so called because of the required four hundred laps around the mile-and-a-half oval, and on race Sunday in May the hours of roaring stock cars sounded like a giant beehive humming in our yard. Fire departments from Charlotte, Concord and Harrisburg, and every country-neighborhood's volunteer fire department drove their trucks and crews – decked out in their yellow and black regalia – to the center field, waiting to exercise their skills if need be. In North Carolina, "Race Fan" is not a label, it's a title. "Race Fans" is not a group, it's a class. And when the splashy first race at Charlotte Motor Speedway ran in 1960, the stock car devotees were a happy lot. Daddy never counted himself among their numbers, but I could tell that he did take satisfaction in his center-field assignments. In fact, he took satisfaction in presuming he had contributed to the track existing at all.

In addition to being a farmer all his life, Daddy also worked in hosiery mills. Those were the "full-fashioned" days, when women's stockings had a seam, a thick, dark line up the center of the leg in the back. Fine nylon filaments were wound on oil-soaked cardboard cones housed on rows of spindled carousels above the long, black iron and brass machines. Once these spools had spent their usefulness in the mill, Daddy brought them home in overflowing greasy cardboard bins to be used as kindling in our fireplace, and God only knows how we lived through the flashes, let alone the fumes.

A knitter, the man operating the machine, fed the filaments through silver rows of hundreds of tiny needles to start the process, and the machine took over. They were sixty-foot monsters creating ear-splitting noise, those machines, giant complexes of pushrods, flywheels, gears, and a thousand and one other bits and pieces, all kept alive by the pungent grease and sweet oil, odors that walked into workers' homes at each shift's end. Each machine created fifteen "legs" at a time, each leg being flat, and the welt, or thick top section of the stocking that would soon hug a woman's thigh, was knitted first. As the stocking developed, it narrowed appropriately to suit the tapering leg of its future home, until finally a heel and foot were formed, and the only thing holding the stocking to the mother machine was an umbilical cord of a single nylon thread.

The knitter – usually operating six machines at a time, three on each side of a wide concrete aisle – would cut the cords, remove the stockings, toss them into a canvas bin in the aisle, and start over. The bin, when full, would be replaced with an empty one before being rolled to another department where the first of hundreds of women would complete the steps to turn the "piece-work" into objects of style and symbols of femininity. Some of them sat at seamers, where they sewed the two outer edges of the leg together, from toe to top, creating the "seam" that made women feel like ladies and made this hosiery be called "full-fashioned." Next, the stockings went to women like my mama: she and others sat in their department, at loopers, with their arms held at shoulder height for eight noisy hours a day, shaped around a thirty-minute "lunch hour." They fed tiny holes over hundreds of fine needles, closer together than piranhas' teeth, and attached the folded-down welt with a "looping stitch" that gave the stocking its tougher, double-thickness top.

Nylon stockings, although made side-by-side, could vary by as much as two inches in length, so the women who worked as pairers handled every leg, sorting them into pairs that were close in length. Another massive room housed the women who made it possible for the eventual contented wearer to end up with silky-feeling legs that were colored taupe, honey, nude, suntan, sandalwood, navy, black or white. Others did the boarding – placing the stocking over a leg-shaped board and steaming it to create the perfect shape that the customer expected to see – and still more women were folders and boxers. The knitters' jobs were mostly automated, the women's, far from it.

Few of the men knew how to repair a serious problem if a knitting machine broke down, so there was a mechanic for each shift, called the fixer. At Hugh Grey, where Daddy worked, the fixer on his shift was a woman – a woman named Katy who had also built her own stone house. She fixed the seamers and loopers as well as the knitting machines and anything else whose greasy, moving parts came to a silent halt. Since Daddy was able to fix most problems that occurred on the knitting machines, he took care of a lot of the glitches himself. He even fashioned some of his own tools to make the job easier and gave some of them to me years later.

His primary job as foreman in the knitting division was to keep the work moving along and make sure the knitters were "meeting production." That is, each job required the worker to produce so many dozens a day. Not dozens of stockings, but dozens of *pairs* of stockings. When a knitter dumped about six "dozen," as it was termed, into the canvas bin, he would signal for the batch to be taken away, and he would log the time and the number of dozens he had produced. Management set the required production numbers – a different number for each department – and wages were based on that minimum. If workers produced more, they were paid more. Of course, if very many workers exceeded the minimum, management would then raise the number, so the employees would race themselves out of a hole only to find they were in a new one because they had done so well. It's no wonder the women were given the same names as their machines: the loopers worked on loopers, the seamers worked on seamers, and so forth, and the men who ran the knitting machines were knitters. They were all human machines.

The first step was a slow one: although the shuttle that carried the yarn shot back and forth across the leg once every second, the longest stocking could be over forty-eight inches long, not counting the foot, which might have added another twelve inches, and the yarn was mighty fine, the leg close-knit. As a stocking was eventually filled with a woman's foot and leg, the length shortened considerably. For its day, the full-fashioned knitting machine was high tech; still, it made only thirty stockings an hour, so if all went well, a knitter could count on no more than sixty dozens a day on his six machines, but things did go wrong and some of the stockings had to be thrown out.

Daddy became suspicious of the numbers being reported by one of the employees under his charge. As time went on, he secretly checked the hose in the man's bin after it had been removed from the end of the man's knitting machine. Days of counting and comparing the numbers with the man's records proved that for every "dozen" recorded, only twenty-two stockings had been dumped, and by the end of his shift, he had given himself credit for producing up to five dozen more than he had actually made. Day after day. Daddy fired him.

Soon after that, this fellow, who had always loved

racing, got together with some other men and they conjured plans that eventually materialized as the great speedway. Daddy says he "gave him his start" by firing him from the mill, and I'm sure Daddy relived those days every time he sat in the middle of that track, waiting for a potentially fiery pileup.

~January 19, 2015~

Chapter 18

Rites of Passage

Don't you just love it when you get tickled where you shouldn't and at something you shouldn't find funny? Happens to my sister and me at family funerals, mainly. It turns an otherwise somber gathering into a freakin' sitcom.

It takes only a look between Lori and me. We know what the other is thinking, and these teeny, tiny little blips of laughter peep out of one and then the other of us and then we start making other noises – like coughing, clearing throats, faking crying – to try to cover up the fact we are laughing at a funeral, for God's sake! This makes it all much worse, of course, and by then we don't dare look directly at each other, but even looking at the other's knee breaks us up, until we laugh out loud at what trouble we're in. I doubt anybody is ever really surprised, however, because there were many funny people in our family who gave us a lot of memories to laugh at, maybe even the one who's lying stone cold dead in front of us.

They started this whole thing, of course; it's their fault. But I'm sitting there about to burst, wishing I

had only farted, and thinking about how much more
fun funerals are than weddings.

~April 21, 2010~

Chapter 19

Skeet

"Skeet" was the nickname reserved for my daddy's sister Nora. When I was a kid I dreaded her arrival for a visit – not because I didn't want to see her, I just didn't like her habit of entry. Upon seeing me, she cackled her raucous laugh and grabbed my face between her two hands, which were tipped with the longest and reddest nails I had ever seen. It was a red matched by her lipstick, which ended up on my face and with a smack right on my lips. Always.

As much as I didn't like that, I loved Skeet, and one of my most precious memories is of her and her baking. She made, undoubtedly, the best chocolate pound cake ever to grace a Cabarrus County oven, and she would bake one and deliver it to me, along with those big, red kisses, every time I came home from college for a weekend. Once, I arrived home and she called.

"Oh, honey, I baked you a cake but I can't bring it to you. It's too sad."

For anyone who doesn't understand that baking term – and maybe it's just a Southern one, I don't know – it means that the cake "fell," which really means it just didn't "rise," as baked things do need to do. I imagine that happened to some cook 'way back and when she took it out of the oven and saw a thick, rather solid instead of fluffy cake, she said, "Oh, that's sad!" and it stuck. To me, this was great news: there should be nothing tastier than a sad chocolate pound cake; it would be like a giant brownie in a tube pan! I begged her to bring it on out to the house, and it was the best chocolate cake I had ever in my life tasted! I'm sure I didn't shut up about it, and Skeet loved that I liked it anyway.

She was so pleased, in fact, that after that, every time she learned I was about to come home for a visit, she would stir up another cake, put it in her oven and then stand in front of the stove and jump up and down, shaking the floor, stove included, so that the cake would fall. So for years after that first one, she continued to bring me "sad" cakes.

There's nothing sad about that kind of love from an aunt.

After years of living with Alzheimer's, she died on November 14, 2009. When I got the news, I could almost smell her chocolate cake.

~November 15, 2009~

Chapter 20

Hold On As Long As You Can

Once in a while, I stumble across a television show I like so much I wish I were friends with the writers. In the summer of 2007, *Lifetime* had a few shows like that, "Side Order of Life" being one of them. In one unforgettable episode, an old woman was in the early stages of Alzheimer's. Her advice to the main character, Jennie, was to hold on as long as you can to all your memories – the good ones and the bad ones – for they all become more precious as they begin to leave.

When I began writing these family stories, I wondered why I was writing so feverishly. I felt I couldn't write fast enough, although I was thinking the stories may never be read by anyone other than my niece and nephew years later, if ever. Meanwhile, I shared a few with my sister and a couple of friends as first drafts were finished because I thought they might find something funny or poignant, and I wondered...and I still do. ...

I wonder if my need to write them might be why the old woman's advice to Jennie struck a chord: because at the time, my daddy had Alzheimer's. So did his sister. And his sister-in-law, my mama's only sister. Two of Mama's brothers died with it.

Alzheimer's is a rampant disease. Standard and expected "forgetfulness" that used to come with old age skips some steps: Alzheimer's is forgetfulness on steroids. It means walking around, but being gone already. Early stages must be horribly sad and frustrating for the one who has it. She may not remember leaving the stove on. She may forget where she parked the car or the route home from church. He may not realize that he pooped in the dog bed in the middle of the night. But there may still be enough understanding left to know to believe the loved one who tells him he did do what he shouldn't have done or didn't do what he should've. I have had to deal with a brain injury myself, so I know for sure that it's no fun at all to feel crazy, in whatever degree.

That so-called early stage is also a very difficult time for the person's family and friends – with constant worry over what might happen next, extra work cleaning up and correcting wrong moves, and an ungodly lack of rest because of necessary and constant vigilance – but, oh, the progression: it never gets easier.

Anyone who has not actually been through it has absolutely no idea what it's like to live with, or to watch closely, the disappearance of the one you love as he or she is replaced by someone you some days experience as an innocent little child, or a mischievous kid, or a mean old coot, or a dangerously mean bitch or bastard, or any or all of them in a single day or hour. Who is it really? I have no idea. I don't have that answer, and I don't know who does.

People who mean well say over and over, "He's still your daddy" or "She's still your aunt." Well, he's not. And she's not. By birth, yes, of course; but that's all. Where does the brain go when it's eaten away by the disease? And what does it bring back to its starving, surviving ridges and gullies from those unknown reaches into oblivion? I don't know if anyone knows, but I do know that when I saw "Daddy" with Alzheimer's, I saw a worn-out, ninety-three year old package that used to hold him. I saw the sad mouth that once poured uproarious laughter when sharing hunting stories with my uncles. I saw the cloudy, searching eyes that used to be bright and clear and twinkled like stars when he thought of something funny to say or do. I saw bent and knobby fingers hanging from bony hands backed with magenta and purple skin, fragile as ancient papyrus. Hands that worked jobs tough as nails – working in a hosiery mill, working a farm, repairing cars and tractors and trucks and lawnmowers, felling trees, building a house. Work that was tender – giving artificial respiration to a new-born puppy whose mama had rolled over and suffocated it but then it lived to make the biggest dog in the litter because of Daddy's healing hands; teaching my young cousins how to fish; holding Lori when he was forty-six and she was just born, and then holding her babies years later; wiping Mama's face with a cool cloth when she was dying of cancer.

Alzheimer's itself is no laughing matter, but once in

a while something funny does happen, and although one feels kind of weird laughing at it, I learned that it is important to latch onto even the slightest tidbit of humor. When Daddy moved out of assisted living and into the Alzheimer's unit, his sister Skeet was already there. Skeet was the resident who never talked except to say, "It's going to be alllllright. ..." She could not pass by a cup, can, or bottle of beverage – no matter whose it was – without picking it up and drinking it. She was almost ninety years old, and I dare say she was more agile than I was, and she rarely sat still for long. Except for a pouchy stomach, her frame was lean, almost lanky. Her face, giving home to bright blue eyes and as many wrinkles as the blue lines on a roadmap, was crowned by a thick batch of white, tousled hair.

My mama's only sister was in the same facility as Daddy and Skeet. Toonsie was only seventeen when I was born, and by the time I reached that age myself, she and I had become great buddies. However, as I kept growing and moved away, accumulating a grocery list of experiences that she couldn't relate to, I remained in her heart and mind the same person I had been as a child, what and whom she wanted me to be. We grew apart, and although I visited her every time I returned home, I felt little if any enjoyment in such a false and, before long, what I could see as only an imaginary connection. I am not the most pragmatic person in the world regarding most aspects of life, but I am when it comes to relationships: they are what they are today; they are not what they used to be. But I loved Toonsie and I always made sure to visit her whenever I went back to North Carolina.

Toonsie continued, right up to her Alzheimer's, to be an uncomplicated person, an avid churchgoer, an all-around good soul, and one to hang onto her privacy. I never knew her to reveal serious feelings, let alone much flesh.

One day one of the attendants took Skeet to the shower and started washing her, only to realize she had not taken everything that she needed into the stall. She must have turned away a wee bit too long, because Skeet escaped. Next thing the staff knew, Skeet was making her usual silent circles in the main living room and dining area, weaving her trail among and around the sofas, recliners, and dining room tables – only this time with added speed – and naked as a jaybird.

Toonsie, relaxing on a sofa, saw her and screamed, "SKEET!! GO PUT SOME CLOTHES ON!!" which only served to cause Skeet to notice where Toonsie was. She went over, plopped her naked self next to Toonsie, and laid her wet, wiry, white head on her shoulder. Toonsie's blouse would have been soaked, except for the fact that she owned nothing that wasn't brittle polyester. The head of nursing, one of the posse chasing after Skeet, said she thought Toonsie was going to have a stroke. I have my doubts that Toonsie had ever seen an equal amount of her own naked self at one time as she saw of Skeet's that afternoon.

Skeet realized that people were close to catching her, so she jumped up, on the move once more. Still, they couldn't stop her because she was too wet and soapy for them to get a grip. She passed the snack cart, grabbed a couple cookies, and kept on going. Soon, someone managed to snatch the cookies out of her hand, but she kept running, them right behind her, one holding a robe, ready to throw it around her.

"Skeet, let us put this robe on you and you can have your cookies back," one of the chasers finally suggested. At that point she stopped dead in her tracks, they robed her, and she ate her cookies.

In our personal world of Alzheimer's, my sister and I were most grateful for the laugh – one more memory for us to hold on to as long as we can, along with all the good and all the bad, holding this one precious until it begins to leave us.

~September 21, 2007~

Chapter 21

Just Five More Minutes

"Monk! What happened to your eye?"

"Oh, Daddy! Please! Not yet – just five more minutes. ..."

It was my usual request, on a Sunday morning like that one, or on any other morning – I loved my "five more minutes" – and I intoned my annoyance that Daddy would use such a dirty trick to get me up.

"You get up and look in the mirror, and if your eye's not gashed wide open, you can go back to bed and sleep till Monday morning!"

I couldn't imagine a better deal, so I got up and stumbled sleepily over to my dresser. To my surprise, above my right eye and below my eyebrow was a horizontal gash, a half-inch long. But no blood. However, the pillow was completely blood-covered. And then, I remembered: I remembered waking during the night, seeing bright red blood all over my pillow case and wondering why Mama had put such a bloody thing on my bed. I had turned the pillow over and gone back to sleep. I walked back to the bed from the mirror and turned the pillow over. Yes, both sides were solid red, both stiff with dried blood!

Mama and Daddy asked me how it happened – that, I didn't remember.

Even at ten I had very hard nails, so we assumed I had perhaps turned over during sleep and cut myself with a fingernail. But with so much blood on the pillowcase, surely there would have been blood under a culprit nail. None. None on my hands, or face, or anywhere. The bed was an old mahogany monster, a mixture of spirals and angles; nowhere on it was there any blood, and had I hit an edge of the bedhead hard enough to cut myself, surely there would have been a bruise. No. No to blood, no to bruise. The only other possible explanation we could come up with was that I had walked in my sleep (which I'd never been known to do) and cut my eye on one of the slats of the blinds that covered the two windows in the room. There was no blood on any of the slats, no blood anywhere on the floor. No blood on the sheets or bedspread. The absolute only blood was on the one pillowcase, but on both sides.

The three of us went to the emergency room instead of Sunday school that day, and the nurse began filling out forms while we waited for the doctor to see me. She asked how it had happened.

"I don't know," I answered truthfully.

"We have no idea," was what she heard from each of my parents when she looked at them, quizzically.

She asked me again, them again, as if the answers would be different if she perfected her questioning.

In 1952, child abuse was not on the tips of all tongues as it is now, but this woman was clearly suspicious. She recorded "unknown" on the lines that should have provided an explanation to the doctor I was soon to meet, but until then she spoke with others behind the desk, in hushed tones and with furtive glances. The doctor gave it his best effort, too, but all we could say, honestly, was that none of us had any idea what had caused the cut.

Four stitches later, we headed home.

It took years for me to develop just enough meager sense to realize the other mystery of that night. Remember that I said I woke up during the night, saw the blood, and turned my pillowcase over? The blinds were tilted for their darkest offering; there were no lights outside the house (we lived way out in the country and no security lights had been installed); no lights were turned on in the room, and I slept with my door shut. Yet I had remembered waking and, in bright light, seeing the bloody pillowcase!

This realization came to me about the same time that I found out that not everyone has the little hard, round knot, or nodule, like I have behind my right ear.

Now, I'm not saying the two are connected – but I'm not saying they aren't.

~January 19, 2015~

Chapter 22

That's the Ugliest Cat...

How many favorite aunts can one niece have? I have
had a few, and one was Daddy's sister Lula, whom
we called Lou. Conjure your notion of what a "real"
Christian person should be, and you just might have
a pretty good picture of Lou. She was one of those
people who read her Bible every morning of her life
– and times in between – sometimes fasted, prayed
incessantly for someone in need, and went to church
every time the doors were open. Frankly, I think she
would've been a good person without all that – and
good she was. She was sweet, she was soft-spoken,
she baked the best yeast rolls I ever ate – and always
baked a fresh buttery batch if she knew I was on my
way over. She was married to George Cline, the first
bald-headed man I ever knew, and her first-born son,
George Wayne, was my make-believe brother. Her
only other child, Ronald, died of leukemia when
he was twenty, I think, and her husband died long
before she did.

Lou knew pain and heartbreak; she knew hard
work on farms, in gardens, in the business she and
my uncle had. Each of their two chicken houses

seemed big as football fields to me. She taught me how to candle eggs on her back porch. She was kind and thoughtful: when Grandma Aldridge (Lou's mother) got so deaf that she couldn't hear the birds singing outside, Lou wedged her cassette recorder in a tree and recorded an hour's worth of birdsong. Grandma kept the recorder on the pillow next to her head and listened to the birds singing every morning before she got out of bed. I think that's just about the sweetest thing anybody could do for another soul.

She was all that – a beautiful woman, a beautiful human being. But pretty, she wasn't. She had worked outdoors since she was a small child, and the labor had weathered and wrinkled her skin; her tanned face was filled with hundreds of tiny lines long before the time she hit fifty.

That's about how old she would've been in 1964, and my little sister was four years old. I was living across the state in Elizabeth City, and one weekend I went home for a visit – and took a tiny kitten to Lori. I didn't ask Mama and Daddy for permission, because I knew what the answer would be; I just took it. The kitty was the kind generally called a tortoiseshell – with all the mangled colors of fall on the farm – but I called it the camouflage kitty. Whatever the correct name of the non-breed creature, for Lori it was furry love, and it made her happy and proud. She walked the house with the purring rag draped over her arm. No surprise then, that when Lou dropped in one day Lori could hardly wait to introduce her new cat to her aunt. Lou looked at the cat for a while, and her mouth dropped open while she tried to think of something nice to say. But Lou was someone who likely found it impossible to tell even a nice, white lie.

"Well, honey, I'm really glad you got a kitty, but honey, well, I hate to say it, but that's the ugliest cat I ever saw. Why, honey, that cat's as ugly as me."

Lori looked at Lou, looked at her cat, looked at Lou again and back at her cat. Then she said to Lou, "Well, that's sure' not sayin' much for my cat!"

~August 29, 2008~

Chapter 23

Christmas Eve, 1954

I sat on the back doorsteps, untying the laces of the calf-hugging hunting boots that my mama had broken in years before. Soon after they married, Daddy had convinced her to go hunting with him and bought her the handsome boots. Now I was twelve years old and it was my turn: my turn to wear the boots, my turn to carry her .410 shotgun, my turn to outshoot my daddy and my uncles and my boy-cousins.

I had left the others a few farms away and walked back to the house, carefully carrying the .410 as I had been meticulously taught, with its bridge open and the shells secured safely in my coat pocket. I loved that gun, and I loved that Daddy had taught me how to shoot so I could go hunting with him. Some folks think of the .410 as a beginner's gun, being small, lightweight and easy to handle, but others think of it as an expert's gun. The small bore allows for a smaller shell, which means a more narrow spray of shot, making hitting the prey a very difficult thing to do, especially if it's on the fly. I, of course, accept the second dubbing, because, after all, I was a very good shot.

In my sock feet, I climbed the five steps to the porch and set the chestnut leather boots in the corner, out of the way. They were cleaned of much of their mud, but not yet perfectly; I would finish cleaning mine when Daddy did his. It would be a way for us to spend time together. What I didn't know then was just how much that time was to be delayed. I placed the shotgun shells from the gun and the extras that were in my pockets in the ammo box on the sill of the screened-in porch. Then I carried the gun into the house, wending my aching feet through the kitchen, around one turn and then another, across my bedroom, and into the hallway near the center of the house.

The aroma of Christmas cakes followed me from the kitchen, sweets that Mama and Grandma Aldridge had baked for the tenant family who lived on the farm; we would bake ours later in the day. However, those plans were about to be changed, because this Christmas Eve wouldn't be like others on Pitts School Road: in a few minutes, George Helton would take the butt of his .22 rifle and split our kitchen door off its hinges.

The hallway was barely longer than it was wide and only a tiny bit bigger than the waffled grid-work cover of the floor furnace. The rotary phone sat perched in the skinny piece of a wall to the right of the bathroom door, like a Black Madonna in a tiny grotto. Still following Daddy's instructions, I left the bridge of the gun open and laid it on the sliver of floor by the furnace grid where it would wait until

114

Daddy came home from the hunt; he was always the one to hang it over the door, straddling it across his handmade rack that was just a little too high for me to reach.

In the kitchen, Mama and Grandma said they needed no help, for me to go into the living room and watch TV for a while. I sat down in Daddy's easy chair, grinning as I thought about him sitting there watching "rasslin'" every week on the tiny black and white screen across the room. He said it relaxed him to watch it, so he'd fix himself in his chair, prepare his pipe with Sir Walter Raleigh cherry tobacco, and pull his pedestal ashtray into place. But his relaxing was short-lived: as soon as things got rough on the screen Daddy sat forward in his chair and puffed harder on his pipe. When his favorite wrestler was at greatest risk, Daddy was on the edge of his seat, restless elbows struggling to connect with his knees. Finally, as his guy was flipped and pinned, Daddy would let out a grunt as loud as the wrestlers' and, without realizing it, turn his pipe upside down. We all scrambled to get the hot ashes off the hardwood floor before any damage was done.

I was sitting there, grumbling to myself that there was nothing on but football, when, in no time it seemed, Mama rushed into the room.

"Quick! Come with me! We've got to hide!"

"What?"

"Don't ask any questions – just come with me!"

I was stunned and confused; my mother never hurried nor did she ever order me to do something. Mama was rushing toward the hallway, aiming for the bathroom, with a neighbor, Lois, right behind her, and Grandma trailing after them. Lois had never been to our house before. Why was she here now, on Christmas Eve, and why was she a member of this abrupt and brisk parade that I was expected to join?

Lois lived a couple miles up the road but I knew her only because she and her husband operated a Citgo service station out by the highway. Her husband had died several months earlier and she had continued to run the business. George Helton had worked there for quite some time, pumping gas, washing windshields, doing odd jobs around the place – and apparently dating Lois since her husband died, although we didn't know that part until later. He had come to the station drunk that day, accusing Lois of two-timing him by dating another one of her employees. She denied the allegations, but George and his liquor were not to be convinced. His threats of killing her began to sound serious – serious enough that she ran to her car to try to get away from him, thinking she just needed to get home. As she was getting into her car, he threw a Coke bottle at her car and shattered a side window. She sped away as he was getting a rifle out of the trunk of his car.

The road to her house took her by ours, and when she saw a dozen cars in our yard – it was a big hunting party that day – she assumed there would be some men there who could protect her from this madman. She was wrong.

"What's happening? What's wrong?" I yelled as I got up from Daddy's chair. None of this – the scenes, the sounds, none of it – made any sense to me. Mama and Lois were rushing ahead of me, but Grandma wasn't moving very fast. Something about her didn't seem quite right, the way she looked, the way she moved.

Lois was the one who answered me. "It's George Helton! He's after me and he's going to kill me!"

When we all reached the heating hall, Mama and Lois went into the bathroom but I pulled Grandma into the doorway to the left, into the bedroom that was in the back corner of the house. She and I could hide behind Mama and Daddy's bed. As I closed the door behind us and turned the lock, I could see my shotgun on the floor in the hallway. I wish I had those shells in here with me: *I could shoot him when he comes toward the bedroom!* But I didn't have them, and as I crouched behind the bed with my arm around my grandma, I remembered that the lock was broken.

"Grandma, follow me! We have to get to the bathroom!" I said, running toward the hall, thinking she was behind me. But she wasn't, and when Mama opened the door and pulled me into the bathroom, we heard the crash of the kitchen door.

Lois was sitting on the bathroom floor, under the window and directly in front of the door, which I thought was more than a wee bit stupid if he had a gun. Mama ordered me to get into the bathtub, into the corner of it far from the bathroom door. Of course, nothing was far from that door; the bathroom wasn't much bigger than the heating hall. She stepped into the tub and pressed herself in front of me. The only semblance of safety between us and the hallway was the space of that tub and Daddy's closet, the one that George Helton might shoot through.

I had not noticed when Lois arrived at the house, and I had been oblivious to the fact that she had been in the hallway calling the sheriff's department while I was only a few feet away, grousing about football. Now, in our implausible hiding place, Mama asked her what had happened and what the cops had said, knowing that if someone didn't come soon, we might all be dead in a matter of minutes.

"They said they don't have anyone available but they'll send someone as soon as they can." As she told us that, George Helton began banging violently on the bathroom door, telling her to come out.

She yelled, "George, I'm not coming out! Go away! There are innocent people in here, and I don't want them hurt!"

"Lois, I've come to kill you, and I'm going to kill you! I'm counting to three: if you aren't out by then, I'm coming in! ONE...TWO..."

And Mama said to Lois, firmly, "Go on out!" To protect me, Mama knew she had to keep George out of the bathroom. Without saying a word, Lois obeyed – she got up and walked out the door. Mama locked the door behind Lois and came back to her spot of protection in front of me. Together we listened to sounds neither of us would ever want to hear again.

In his drunken frenzy, George Helton beat Lois Poplin to a bloody pulp. He broke her ribs. He knocked out her teeth. He stomped her head against the furnace grate, cutting her face. And he gave her a concussion. Her blood was splattered all over the bright white enamel of Daddy's closet door, and the little square of hardwood floor in front of it held a pool of crimson about two feet wide. There was blood all over my shotgun on the floor. About chest high in the wall above my gun there was an eight-inch hole in the sheetrock, caused by his fist or her head or the butt of his gun bashing through it.

In the bathtub, shielded by my protective mother, separated from a life-and-death struggle only by a thin door and a small, crowded closet of clothes, the mesh of cries and screams and thuds and cursing was almost deafening. Then, all of a sudden, there was silence. I'm sure Mama and I both thought Lois was dead, that certainly we would be next. But in that momentary calm, we heard a car pull up in the back yard and the sound of one car door shutting, then another. But it wasn't the cops.

Daddy was a hosiery mill foreman in those days, and the mill had a policy that employees were not to give gifts to their supervisors. However, the workers loved Daddy, and one man always ignored the rule

119

and each year at Christmas gave him a present. Bob had arrived with that year's gift – and with his two-year-old son in his arms. When he walked up the steps and onto the porch, he saw the destroyed door, smelled the freshly baked cakes, and saw no sign of Mama or me. Well, who wouldn't figure something was really wrong? Still carrying his little boy, Bob turned the corner from the kitchen, stepped into my bedroom, and ran smack-dab into George Helton, holding Lois in a chokehold with one arm, the rifle in his other hand. Pointing the gun at Bob's little boy's face, George told Bob to get out. Bob asked where we were, and Lois managed to tell him we were okay, that we were in the bathroom. He didn't say a word; he just turned around, took his son back to the car, and told him to stay there until he got back.

As Bob approached the steps on his way back into the house, George appeared on the top step and aimed the gun directly at him. While Bob was trying to persuade George that he was already in enough trouble and should hand over the rifle, Lois scrambled her broken self together, ran out the other end of the house, and hid in some bushes. For some reason, George relinquished the gun, and Bob started discharging the bullets. Before the last one was ejected, George started to jump him – and Bob slammed the bullet back into its chamber.

"You son of a bitch, you come one step closer to me and I'll blow your goddamn head off!"

Through the bathroom window, Mama and I saw the deputies finally pull into the back yard. They loaded George and Lois – both of them – into the back seat of the car. She had to ride to town right beside the man who had nearly beaten her to death. Our neighbors Alice and Millie saw them leave, and they brought Grandma back home. As George had turned toward the bathroom door, Grandma had sidled past him and managed to escape to Millie's house across the road.

Bob and I went in his car to search for Daddy, stopping frequently to yell out the window, me yelling "Daddy! Daddy!" and Bob yelling "Luther! Luther!" We didn't find him, but Bob filled me in on what had happened after he arrived at the house. While we were gone, Alice and Millie got Grandma into my bed. They looked out my bedroom window and saw the hunters ambling up the lane from the back of the farm. Alice ran to meet Daddy.

"Get to the house right now! Quick! Your mother needs you!"

Daddy handed his .12-gauge shotgun over to my uncle and ran to the house. He didn't even notice the deep splits in the kitchen door or the deadbolt lock half way across the kitchen floor, its screws bent like elbows. What he did notice was his mother, grey as a ghost, sprawled on her back on my bed in the room just off the kitchen, with Millie rubbing her arms frantically, waiting for the doctor to arrive and declare that, yes, she *had* suffered a heart attack. He noticed the pool of blood in the hall, the hole in the wall, my now-closed and bloody gun on the floor, and no sight of his wife or daughter. Daddy assumed I had tried to put the gun in the rack and that it had gone off and killed Mama or me, and that Grandma had seen it happen and suffered a heart attack.

Mama firmly believed that if she couldn't say something nice about someone she shouldn't say anything at all, and she tenaciously adhered to her conviction. But when she came out of the bathroom that day with towels to clean up the mess of blood and teeth left in the aftermath of the sheer evil that had tainted our Christmas Eve and Daddy asked her what had happened, she simply said, "That Devil. ..." It was the only time she ever said such a thing about anyone.

One afternoon before the trial began, I was in the yard when a strange woman drove up, two young boys in the back seat of her station wagon. She told me she wanted to see my daddy so I went into the house to get him. It was George's ex-wife and she had come to ask Daddy to drop the charges he had filed because she needed the alimony.

"Too bad!" Daddy said as he turned brusquely and walked into the house, with me following along.

Even though I was young, I knew I needed something to lessen the brutality of the experience that was burned in my memory, and I felt that experiencing the process of justice would ease the imagery I constantly carried. No matter how much I begged my case, Daddy would not allow me to go to the trial. Perhaps his decision was equally influenced by his usual tendency to be overprotective and his concern over what he might say and how he might behave in the courtroom. After all, when Mama had told him what "that devil" had done, even though Daddy was standing by our phone in the hallway, he turned to Alice and asked if he could use hers. He drove up the hill to her house, walked in the back door directly past her husband (whom he never noticed), went straight to their phone, and called the sheriff's department.

"This is Luther Aldridge. Do you have George Helton locked up?"

"Yes, we do."

"Well, you'd better *keep* him locked up, because if he ever sets foot on my land again, I'll kill him!"

During and after the trial, my parents wouldn't tell me what went on in the courtroom. Lois had not even filed any charges. She probably knew that if she in any way helped send him to prison, he wouldn't get much of a sentence, and that he would surely kill her when he got out. So, "justice" meant that George Helton got a nine-month suspended sentence. Those were chain-gang days, and he served as a cook "on the road" for two weeks before he was released. Breaking and entering and attempted murder. Go figure.

Our family spoke of the entire affair way too little, I think. I overheard Daddy and Bob talking about it once, but I don't remember Mama ever bringing it up again. Certainly not in front of me.

Before school reopened after the holidays, our local

paper ran the story, an entire page, about what had transpired, and Lois and her boys were named. I was always concerned about those little boys, both younger than I. When I got on the school bus the first day it came 'round, I saw them sitting together with their heads dropped. I was so worried that their classmates would tease them, because I'm sure most families would've read that Sunday paper, and I told my mother I was worried about them.

Her only response was, "I'm sure they'll be okay." Then, never another word from her about it. I have always wondered how many ways they might have been affected.

I don't know how Lois's life turned out after that; I never saw her again. I avoided the Citgo station like the plague and rode my bike to the store on the other corner because I thought she would be embarrassed if she had to face me. A couple years later the station had new owners.

The trauma of some strange man coming into our house to kill another person whom we barely knew would prove enough to cause me nightmares, and that pool of blood by the furnace grate provided the visuals. For months afterward, I would lie in bed at night, finally reaching far enough away from the conscious memory of the horror to find sleep, only to see in the unwelcome darkness of dreams washes of blood streaming down my bedroom walls.

~September 22, 2007~

Chapter 24

Well, Blow Me Down!

"Well, blow me down!"

Hard to tell just how many times I ever heard my
daddy say those words. Whenever he heard or saw
something he thought to be unbelievable, he'd
almost always say, "Well, blow me down!" and then
proceed to explain why he was so surprised, sometimes adding his own story that somehow connected
the current shock to his own experience. So it was
fitting, I suppose, that I received the news while
standing – barely standing – on a mesa outside Las
Cruces, New Mexico, pumping gas into my RAV4,
in a wind that nearly blew me down.

I had left my home in Tucson that Wednesday
morning, October 17, 2007, thinking I would make
it back in time, back "Home." Does a near-sixty-
five-year-old woman from Rhode Island or Iowa
or Michigan or Nevada still call the place she lived
with her parents "Home?" I wonder if it's a Southern thing. I don't know about those women, but
I do know that in my case, at least, it's as inbred
as my accent is: a natural, automated preservation
and perpetuation of a dutiful, even respectful title,

diving deep as a tap root through time to the house, the address, the county, the state, and to the people there. No matter how long and far away I have wandered from those earlier years and places, I still say "Home." With a capital H.

My sister and I had already talked a few times that day, but as I pulled off of I-10 and toward the rows of gas tanks standing like Big Oil's kachinas in this ancient landscape, the cell rang again.

"Hi!"

"He's gone."

"Who's gone?"

I had been so certain: I would finish this four-day journey on Saturday night, rolling over the two-thousand mark on the meter-miles as I pulled into Lori and Jim's drive. Then it would happen probably two days later. I was sure of it. I had said goodbye to him God-only-knows how many times in the last maybe fifteen years. He was always there next time. His mama was like that. She never expected to see you again when you left her. I catch myself lately saying something she said for as long as I knew her – and she lived to be a hundred – "If I live. ..." Except that she said it as though she probably wouldn't, and if you left now, you just might never see her again. *And* you just might be sorry later that you didn't stay longer now.

But it didn't happen that way. I had left Tucson on Wednesday morning; it was now only Wednesday afternoon. It was not Saturday night, I was not in my sister's driveway in North Carolina, I was not going to get to hold his hand one more time even though he wouldn't know I was doing it, and I was not believing I was hearing that question come from me: *"Who's gone?"*

I had been so certain.

~April 21, 2008~

Chapter 25

Things That Go Bump

My daddy saw ghosts. His mama was a hundred years old when she died in 1995, and the last fifteen years of her life, at least, were nothing any of us wish for. But she had always said she wanted to live to be a hundred, and by God, she got her wish. She should have added some phrase about quality of life while she was wishing. Soon after she died, Daddy was lying in bed one night and he said a window appeared on the wall beyond the foot of his bed. Outside the "window" appeared a beautiful day – bright sky, flowers, a gentle breeze rustling the trees – and Grandma walked by the window from right to left. When she reached mid-window, she turned and gave him a great smile. He vowed he wasn't asleep.

He told me a few stories of unusual – and unexplained – sights and sounds that he had begun to experience as a young boy. His sister Lou saw some of the same things at the same time, so Daddy said he knew they didn't just come from his imagination. One of the stories involved an old blue tick hound that strolled into their front yard while he and Lou

were sitting on the porch late one summer afternoon. The old dog looked at them, heisted his leg as
if to pee on the tree, looked at them again, and then
– poof! It disappeared into thin air. Daddy casually
asked Lou, "Did you see that?"

"Yep."

"Me, too."

And that was that, he said. No dog. No pee on the
tree. No paw prints in the dirt.

When Daddy was young there was a common look
and layout to country houses: from the front porch
of the unpainted clapboard homes, a person would
enter the front door into a hallway that went all the
way through the house to the kitchen at the back
end, and the kitchen led to the back porch. But in
the front part of the house, there were rooms off the
hallway, and usually the first one on the right was
what we would now know as a living room. Back
then though, for people of means, the room probably would have been called a parlor. For people like
my daddy and his family and friends, it was the sittin' room. It's where family sat together after a hard
day of work, where company was enjoyed. It was
where wakes were held, and it was where people sat
soberly awaiting Death to come to a sick member of
the family.

I don't recall if the old codger he told me about
was a relative or just someone his family knew, but
Daddy described him as a despicable person who
had been sick for quite a while, and everyone knew

his days were shortening. Daddy remembered being in that sitting room as a young boy the night of the old man's last minutes on earth.

Everyone was sitting quietly, so quietly that they could hear the old man's labored breathing and death rattle coming from the room directly across the hall. Then they heard something else. It sounded like a logging chain, he said, being dragged up the several steps to the porch, sliding across the porch. The screen door squeaked, the sound of the dragging chain came the short way down the hall to the old man's doorway, turned, and judging by the time the sound continued, it slid to the side of his bed. There was a scream, and the dragging chain sounded its way out of the house just as it had come in. Family members ran into the man's room and found him dead.

Daddy had no qualms about relating these stories, at least not to me. But there was other family information carefully protected by silence. Stories not of ghosts but of skeletons. My sister and I talk about some of them, and about how reluctant our family was to name the truth of a circumstance.

Lori tells of eventually sitting around our dining room table with Daddy and Lou – I don't know who else might have been there – and hearing stories of the Big Three Family Sins, although no one would name them as such. I guess if you don't name it, it's not nearly as bad a sin, and maybe not one at all.

I had asked about Grandma Aldridge's daddy a

lot when I was growing up, but I didn't get any satisfactory answers. I would hear a few stories about her with her mother, but never anything about her father. For many years, the most I got was the clipped, "Well, she never knew her daddy." But that wasn't completely true. Eventually, Daddy did tell me more of the story: turned out that our great-grandma and a rather well-heeled married man begat the child that grew up to be my Grandma Aldridge. Daddy knew his name, his wife's name, where they had lived, that he was a fine man, and one who kindly "did the best he could by them." Apparently, he visited them often when Grandma was young and gave them bits of money, but I don't think that attention lasted very long because even when she was quite young, Grandma, carrying a wooden box to stand on, went around with her mother to wash dishes and clean houses for other people in order to make a living. As disgustingly inappropriate as the word is, Daisy Aldridge was "illegitimate." When telling Grandma's story, her son and daughter said, "Well, no – she wasn't illegitimate – she just didn't have a daddy." And the word adultery was never uttered.

Neither was bigamy. Grandpa Aldridge had a brother who lived in North Carolina but the need for work led him to Virginia. He met a woman there, married her, and had a slew of kids. Mind you, he still had a wife and family back in North Carolina. When the first wife found out there was a second wife, she went to Virginia to retrieve her husband. She packed him up, along with his new spouse and new children, brought them all back home, and made him take care of all of them.

God, I wish I could have known her!

Another one of our illustrious ancestors who lived around Cottonville, North Carolina got into a fight one night with some of his cousins. The fight heated up to the point that a knife was pulled, and, as Daddy told the story, our relative slashed out at one of the other boys and "his guts fell out all over his shoes." He ran home and told his mama what he had done. She packed his things and told him to keep running. Every time the sheriff questioned her, she would only tell him she didn't know where her son was – which, of course, was the truth. Daddy said they later had reason to believe he had ended up in Oklahoma.

But if you don't call it murder...

~March 7, 2009~

Chapter 26

The Gravity of Life

There wasn't much bathroom privacy in our house among the female members, and one night I was standing at the lavatory brushing my teeth when Grandma Aldridge came in, wedged past me, pulled up her dress-tail, as she would call it, and sat down to pee. She sat there for a bit in silence, highly unusual for Grandma, 'cause she talked or sang incessantly. Maybe she was pondering aging, because when she did speak, she said to me, "Do you know when you get older you go bald down there?"

"What?"

"When you get old, you go bald down there."

"Oh, Grandma, you do not!"

"Yes, you do!" – and she lifted her dress and showed me her crotch, bald as a baby's butt.

That should have been a warning to me but it wasn't. A warning to pay attention to life, to years, to changes, to inevitability, I suppose. Therefore, one night I went to bed at age forty-five and when I woke up I was twenty years older and had paid little attention to the time between.

I've never felt ownership of my body. Disconnected somehow. I really don't know whether to be sorry about that or not. I mean, I have friends who seem so body-obsessed that I wouldn't want to trade places with them, but still – who is this that I live inside? Or what?

I mean, it is functional, not as much as it used to be, granted, but until about four years ago it did serve me somewhat decently. Until then, I was in good shape – if a pear is a good shape, or if round is a good shape. Yes, if I could have managed to lose about a fourth of myself, I might once again have enjoyed tying tennis shoes or trimming toenails or climbing ladders or getting down on the floor and up again or going for walks or playing tennis. None of those things were fun anymore and some were painful. Now that I am partially paralyzed, things are very different, but that's another story.

I can remember when I started college in 1960: I was a five-foot-nine-inch beanpole and weighed a hundred and twenty-eight pounds. I lay on the beach at Nags Head, lifted my head to look at the ocean, and gazed across a distinct triad of hip and pubic bones. I haven't owned those bones in years. They were traded in for what my nurse-cousin Ellen informed me is an "abdominal apron." It's sort of like the midriff spare tire that slips down toward one's crotch and just hangs around, waiting for nothing. Handlebars on a low rider. When I was skinny, narrow shoulders – which I got from both parents, I guess – were no big deal. But now, I'm a food pyramid with legs.

But I must back up a minute. When I said I paid no attention for twenty years, there was one thing I did notice at forty-five. When I blew out the candles on that cake, I deflated any perkiness that was left in my breasts. Suddenly they were lying on my belly. Back in the perkier days, my left breast was always bigger than the right one; now it's just longer. Even this is not a bad thing, which may come as a surprise to my friends who still bask in a brisk bounce of some firmness. I've always imagined body parts as being useful in unexpected ways, and years ago as I gained weight and my belly button became deeper, I used to tell people that I could store all my earthly possessions in my belly button. That was before my house became a likely project for one of Oprah's de-hoarding crews.

Now you might guess that, as a general rule, I will not be found in a bathing suit except in very rare circumstances. That's way too near naked for public consumption. However, when I am in bed or at home alone, al fresco suits me just fine. When I go to bed, I use my cell phone as an alarm clock. One morning I got up, did all my bathroom duties, and decided to check my email before showering. One thing led to another, hours passed, and I decided to make a long distance call before showering, but I couldn't find my cell phone. I looked everywhere: by the bed, in the bed, under the bed – which I've already told you is not an easy thing to do – in the bathroom, by the computer. It never occurred to me to use the house phone to call the cell phone and chase down the sound. Had I done that, it probably would've scared the wits out of me, because I had been carrying the thing around all that time tucked under my left breast. I have a lot of friends who can't dream of accomplishing such a thing.

Grandma and her bald butt lived to be a hundred. I have no interest in living that long. I know if I were to, I'd be tripping all over my dangling boobs.

~August 16, 2008~

Chapter 27

Embers

In the place where Time isn't, there is a giant ball of fire. Well, maybe it's not fire, maybe it's Light. And maybe it's not Light, maybe it's just Energy. Maybe it's not even that; maybe it's Nothing At All, but it is as however it sees fit. Or maybe it's more like however it agrees to create itself, but that would imply there's something greater than that Big Ball of Whatever, wouldn't it? Maybe that's true, maybe not. If it is true, maybe that Bigger Whatever is what we have been told is God. It probably doesn't matter a whit, really, whether there's a shred of truth or even possibility in all of this, but my mind insists on picturing something, and what it sees is a big chunk of illuminated oomph that is so creative it just can't help but burst wide open!

So it does.

Smaller chunks break off and streak away; still smaller pieces explode from those, on and on and on. In my mind's moving picture, it's those flying embers that become us, us bipedal human creatures on this planet. That's the stardust that we are. In my mind.

I've long thought of myself – and I think of you this way, too, by the way – as one of those second-level illuminations. Let's just say, for the sake of numbers, that a second-level chunk breaks into half a dozen pieces. I think, just maybe, that I – as the person saying this right now – am one of those pieces; the other five are scattered here and there on Earth, and we are all segments of our one illumination. In other words, I am six people and each of my other selves is six people. I think of that on days when I feel something has gone terribly wrong although there is no evidence in my local existence of anything having happened to create such overwhelming sadness or fear. Has something, in fact, happened to one of my sextuplets and that is what I'm sensing? At times when I experience such depression that I describe it as "terminal sadness," has one of them died? Has that "part of me" disappeared?

I was driving from Toledo, Ohio to Bowling Green one day along a stretch of I-75 that was as familiar to me as my own face. You know how it is on a drive like that. You "come to" after a bit, perhaps you've traveled ten miles virtually on autopilot: you have no sense of the space or time covered in those lost minutes and you're just grateful that you didn't kill yourself or somebody else while you were paying absolutely no attention to what you had been doing – driving! That particular day, I was aware of where I had "come back from." I had experienced, as plain as day, sitting in a diner in a sparsely populated desert area of Arizona. Mind you, at that time I had never been to Arizona, nor had I even thought about going there. I could see clearly the clothes I was wearing (cowboy clothes – striped shirt, dark blue jeans, black boots with some silver studs on them); I could describe the woman across the table and the booth we sat in by the window. Hell, I could describe how the place smelled, what the vinyl seat felt like! I saw it all, felt it all, I was aware of it all – just as if I were really there! – except that I could not see my face, nor could I identify my gender. I doubt anyone will ever convince me that I was not there, experiencing – no, *being!* – one of my other selves.

You don't have to say it's crazy; I know it seems that way.

Another thing that fascinates me about us flying sparks is this: whenever I meet someone with whom I feel an instant connection, I know that I am meeting another "ember" from the third-level chunk of energy (counting back toward the Source) from which I, too, came. Those discoveries are our so-called soul mates, our heart buddies, our sisters and brothers of no blood kin (or in some fortunate cases, like mine with my sister, we may also be earthly related). I have a few friends of thirty years or more who fit that bill. Lately, I have been meeting people, new to me here, who are undoubtedly identifiable to me as "fellow sparks."

Crazy or not, I am the most fortunate of creatures and grateful for these gifts of recognizable stardust embers who are entering my life.

ENDNOTE: A day after I wrote this, author Eckhart Tolle posted on Facebook, "The universe has conspired to put you here. The totality of all the molecules and atoms that are floating around the universe, some of them temporarily gathering together and manifesting what looks like a person. They were forged in the furnace of stars and in this amazing way it's all coming together; the totality of life has suddenly put you here. Everything is connected to everything else, it's all timeless."

~May 8, 2010~

Chapter 28

Elevator to the World

Did you know that most of Emily Dickenson's poems can be sung to the tune of "The Yellow Rose of Texas"? I am thinking of her because she lived and died in the same house where she was born. During her adult life, she seldom even left the house. Maybe she tired of everyone breaking into song when she hit the streets.

No one will ever report such stability – if that's what it might be – regarding my life. I've lived a lot of places, and everywhere I've lived, I've lived at least twice. Well, that is enough true that it is a near-fact of amazing significance. To me it is, anyway. I mean, don't you agree it's really odd? Trying to name every town now, at my age, is rather like trying to name every lover. Some place or some body is bound to be overlooked. But I shall try. The places, that is; don't get your hopes up about the other list.

Concord, Sanford, Concord, Harrisburg, Greenville (returning each fall for four years), Hertford, Elizabeth City, New York City (two summers), Elizabeth City, Lumberton, Harrisburg, Lumberton, Bowling Green (OH), Harrisburg, Charlotte, Harrisburg,

Charlotte, Bowling Green, now Tucson. To make figures worse, just starting with Bowling Green Number One through my third year in Tucson – that would be 1979 to 1994 – my cat JB and I moved fifteen times until she died in '94. I worry that I wore her out.

I get memory-flashes of the places I lived in these various towns, and sometimes one particular place "relives" in my memory for days. I wonder why that is. Lately, I've been reliving Location Number Two in Elizabeth City Number Two.

It was 1968 and I had quit my job in New York City, returned to E-City to work with Virginia Electric and Power Company as their little Martha Stewart before there was a Martha Stewart, and for a short while I lived in a homey little motel that could be rented by the month. Finally, I found an apartment, half of the upstairs of a sparkly white Victorian house on oak-lined Main Street. The old man and woman whose home it had been for their entire married life were long dead, and their daughter, who lived downstairs, was my landlady. She told me that her sister lived in the other apartment that comprised the rest of the upper half of the house. She was a mystery then as well as now: I never once laid eyes on her. Maybe she was a poet. All else I was told was that entry to the sister's apartment was through the downstairs residence; my entrance would be from the back.

Via a freight elevator.

The elevator shaft was butted up to the side of the

144

landlady's garage that sat a good distance from the back of the house; at the top, there was what amounted to a breezeway, half closed in, that slanted from the elevator upward to my kitchen door. The reason for this arrangement, I was told, was that the old man had been in a wheelchair during his last years and to reach the second floor of the home where the bedrooms were, he, of course, had to have an elevator. He didn't have the luxury of useful legs, but the family did have the luxury of lots of money; elevators weren't cheap. Still, this one was nothing fancy.

It looked like it had come from an Army Surplus Store: heavy steel, painted drab Army green. I was still young and had not yet developed Ovaries of Steel that give women the courage to ask for what we need, let alone want. I did not want to go and come in Army Drab a minimum of twice a day, but I couldn't bring myself to ask if it would be okay to paint it purple, or gold – or emerald green, at least. Instead, I bought travel posters of every country or city I could find that boasted life as colorful! bright! happy! and I slathered the walls and ceiling with as much paper-happiness as humanly possible. It was a Good Thing.

While traipsing around the eastern two-thirds of the USA for The McCall Pattern Company, I had had time to shop in cities with fascinating stores, chains that wouldn't reach my home-turf of the South for years. Sears, JCPenney, and Belk were just about the best we had to offer. But, oh, in Detroit, in Minneapolis, in Kansas City (where the first strip

145

mall was born!), not to mention New York, oh boy, oh boy! I would discover placemats, table runners, candlesticks, specialty dishes, dish cloths – now, how different would you think dish cloths could have been? But they were! And I would buy myself these gorgeous things and have them sent back home with a note saying, "Mama, please save these for me until I need them."

Finally, I needed them. They added interest, I probably thought a bit of class, to the rest of my apartment that was filled with what amounted to Early Salvation Army decor. It was actually worse than that. Two end tables were fabric-draped wooden cable spools discarded by the power company after the men had strung the lines across the countryside. My bedroom suite was bought from the assorted belongings of a dead woman. It came to me dark brown; it lived with me as Chinese red, black trim.

The head of that bed backed up to the wall of the living room, so the sofa was right behind my head when I slept. Beyond the living room was the kitchen, beyond that, the breezeway, and then the Elevator to the World. These were huge rooms, so my bedroom would have been a long way from the back yard, if there had been one. There wasn't, but there was that garage with a short paved drive toward it from the side street and, beyond a bit of grass, a neighbor's house.

One summer night, a Saturday hot as all get-out, my windows were up, I was in bed reading and trying to pretend I wasn't so miserably hot. Over the din of the fans going, I heard what sounded like a man crying. That's not a sound easy to ignore. I pressed my head to the window screen and determined that whatever I was hearing was coming from the back of the house. There was no quiet way out of my apartment, but I put on my clothes and headed for the elevator. From the breezeway I could see what appeared to be, barely bathed in streetlight, a young man sitting on the driveway, his feet in the street, his head in his hands, bawling like a baby.

I'm fifty years older now, and during those years the world seems to have become meaner than it was then; I've been scared a number of times, and I've seen hatefulness that has nearly stopped my heart, human viciousness that can only be called barbaric. As much as I dislike admitting it, if what I saw then were happening now on a sweltering hot Saturday night, or, worse, perhaps any time at all, I would probably watch the guy and feel sorry for him – at a maintained distance of safety. But, as I said, fifty years ago things were different. And so was I. My heart went out to that stranger whose own heart surely seemed broken: it was one of those too-rare occasions when I have felt, truly, "I am you, you are me."

I doubt he even heard the god-awful grinding of the elevator as it delivered me to the ground. I walked over to him and laid my hand on his shoulder. His swollen eyes looked into mine, and for a moment he stopped sobbing. No matter how dumb the question, we always open with it: "Are you okay?"

He finally got some words together. He had been next door at a party all day; the people he had come with had left early; he had expected to get a ride back to the Coast Guard base outside of town, but he had gotten really drunk and had fallen asleep; everyone else had left, he didn't even know the hosts, now he was AWOL because he had missed his midnight curfew. He was embarrassed, he was ashamed of being so irresponsible, and he was scared to death of what he would have to face when he arrived at base. I offered to drive him out there. He said he couldn't show up drunk – that would make matters even worse. It was then that I said, "Come on – you're going to sleep this off upstairs," and draping one of his arms around my neck and holding him tightly around the waist, I led him to the elevator without either of us taking a tumble and propped him in the corner between Spain and Italy.

Upstairs, I took him directly to the sofa. He was no longer crying, just thanking me over and over. I was only seven years older than this nineteen-year-old Coastie, a young man who had volunteered to serve our country, yet sitting in my living room was simply a frightened little boy. Although I never touched him, except to help him upstairs, I knew and he knew that he was being held, wrapped in honest caring and a loving embrace. He spilled much of his brief life story – and then barely made it to the bathroom to spill the rest of his day. I gathered bedding for the sofa and prepared it for his short sleep. I found a new toothbrush and handed it through the bathroom door and prepared the coffee pot for him to turn on when he woke. Then I told him I would be just on the other side of the wall from him, for him to pound on it if he needed anything; I would give him a ride, come morning. I crawled into bed, turned out the light, and only then did it cross my mind, "This could be dangerous." But by then there was nothing that could follow that thought except, "Oh, well," and I went to sleep.

His morning came much earlier than mine. He had likely hitched a ride to base before I ever saw the light of day. He was probably already facing his superiors and preparing himself for his due punishment. What I was facing were neatly folded linens and one of the most beautiful and loving notes anyone had ever given me. I wish I had kept it.

~June 19, 2009~

Chapter 29

Down on the Farm

I had a friend who grew up in New York. She probably felt as much at home dodging Manhattan traffic as navigating the produce aisle in a grocery store, and she was fascinated by the fact that I grew up on a farm. What fascinated me was that someone who knew virtually nothing about a farm could ask so many questions about it. I don't mean that it was annoying, I mean that it was amazing. I think of myself as a rather inquisitive person, but I see that my curiosity is not particularly creative – or broad. Mine has always had the bent of the philosophical, questions that either have no answers, or if they do, they are hard to articulate, and if they are articulated, somebody's probably going to end up using them to start a war or two. But on the less aggressive side, while my friend would likely ask, "What was it like to grow corn on your farm?" I would probably ask, "Why does corn exist?"

We did grow corn. We also grew wheat, alfalfa, milo, cotton, and cows. We had chickens, pigs, hunting dogs and pet dogs. There was a distinct difference between the two: Daddy didn't think hunting dogs should be treated like pets, and his treatment of them was not admirable by my standards; the closest he came to being kind to them was to give them food and water and names like Betty and Lucy and Millie. Although if I had had time during my hard-core-Feminism years to remember the treatment and the girls' names, I probably would have created some associations that I would not have been happy about.

While Grandma Aldridge was living with us on the farm, she wanted some critters of her own, so Daddy built a little enclosure and shelter and drove Grandma to the feed store to pick out her baby bantams. Most people call baby chicks baby chicks; we called them peepies. If you don't know what a bantam is, but you do know what a chicken is – in real life, not in styrofoam and plastic wrap – just imagine a miniature chicken. That's pretty much it, just a small breed. Thing is, the little rascals can be aggressive, I guess to make up for their small size. Like bantam-weight boxers. Or George W. Bush. Anyway, Grandma loved those chickens and she tended them with lavish care from little peepies to full-grown miniature chickens. I reckon they loved her, too, because she would let them out of the pen and they would follow her around like puppies. Her chickens taught me something I never would have known had I not lived on a farm: a rooster has to learn how to crow. Her little bantam boy, before too long, began to look like the cock of the walk he was destined to become, but for quite a while, whenever he opened his beak to proclaim his developing pride, he was to be nothing but pitied. The "crow" began with three amply strong syllables, "Errrr-err-errrr –" but trailed off with a weak "krrhhruuu" that sounded like a death rattle. That rooster might have repaid Grandma's love in like kind, but I also learned that it's quite possible that chickens hold grudges: I had laughed at that little rascal way too many times, and I suffered the pecks to prove it.

Everything we grew on the farm was to put food on the table – except for the cotton, of course, and that did, indirectly, when it was sold. We had plenty of eggs from the chickens: regular eggs from regular chickens, the Rhode Island Reds, and teeny ones from the bantams. They were barely half the size of the eggs everyone is accustomed to, and they had a very dark yellow yolk and a stronger taste. The bigger chickens were sacrificed to the Table Gods out in the back yard now and then. The first time I ever saw my grandma "wring a chicken's neck" and then chop its head off, I never wanted to see it again. Nor did I again want to smell the odor of holding the carcass over a fire to burn off the stubble that was left after the feathers were plucked. Want to or not, once you've known that stink, simply remembering it brings it back. I have no idea why I'm not a vegetarian, except that selective memory and taste buds rule.

But killing a chicken was nothing compared to killing a hog. There weren't many of those days, thank god.

We had one old hog that was humongous, even as hogs go. She must've weighed at least six hundred pounds. We never had a riding lawn mower so big.

One afternoon, soon after I had come home from school and Mama had gotten home from work, someone called and asked if we had a pig on the loose. The fat old lady had rooted out of her pen and was wandering around on Pitts School Road in front of our house. Mama called Daddy at the mill to ask if he could come home and put the ol' hog back in her pen, and he told us to take a rope and try to round her up before he got there. Before long – even though it seemed like an eternity – Daddy came home and the hog was returned to her sty, but for the life of me I've never remembered how it happened. My only complete memory of the day is chasing the pig: there we were, a nine-year-old girl and her thirty-five-year-old mother, in the sweltering Carolina summer heat, running into the sun for the length of two football fields of asphalt, trying to catch up with that damn hog who was trotting her fat ass right along the yellow line as if to prove her sobriety and control.

"What do we do if we catch her?" I asked Mama, in between gasps.

There's no guarantee that "Here, piggy, piggy" is going to work on a six-hundred-pound creature who wanted to get away in the first place, and I for sure didn't want to be the one to let her know I was holding a rope intended for her neck. I thought country ham with red-eye gravy was way overrated anyway, so it seemed fine to me if she waddled on over the hill to a new and longer life somewhere else.

Ever after, that hog and I eyed each other warily

154

whenever I carried the slop can down to feed her after our supper. And while I didn't particularly trust – or even like her, for that matter – neither did I enjoy seeing her killed later that fall.

Daddy suffered for years with recurring problems from slipped discs in his back. More than once he would be down at one of the sheds, and his back would catch him; he'd fall to the ground and literally claw himself back to the house, to be in bed for days. When hog-killin' time rolled around that year, he was "down in his back" again. Grandma Aldridge, a farming woman from way back, was there to help; Grandma Helms, who I don't think ever lived on a farm, but I do think knew just about everything there was to know, was there; so were uncles, who were there to do the most dastardly deeds of killing and hanging the monstrous animal – with the help of the tractor – and slitting her neck and then her underside from stem to stern(um). Grandma Helms tended the big black cauldron that was set up right by where the pig hung, and she stirred the stuff, the chitterlings, or "chitt'lins," that they pulled out and cooked in the huge kettle. I have to say, smelling a singeing chicken is almost sweet compared to that hot vat, wide-open hog, and a big tin tub of raw entrails. I have to say, too, that one good reason for growing up and moving away from a farm is that rarely if ever does one have to say the word "entrails."

Mama had been raised a "city girl," and this was her first experience with killing hogs. Mine, too, of course. While she and Grandma Aldridge managed kitchen duty, I was doing as little of this nasty work as I possibly could get by with, glad that it was considered adult work. Daddy was flat on his back in bed in the bedroom that was directly off the kitchen. A cast iron meat grinder was attached to the kitchen counter, and Grandma Aldridge was busy trying to keep up with the deliveries of meat brought to her, feeding it into the grinder, steadily turning the crank for hours, while huge ropes of sausage exited the machine, stuffing itself into the well-washed intestine casings Grandma kept attached to the spout. And people wonder why I don't like to eat link sausage.

My charge was to fetch, as they were readied, big pots of the old hog's fat and carry them to Mama, who was waiting at the kitchen stove. That was the first step in rendering that all-important cooking staple, lard, and rendering the lard was one of the most important aspects of hog killing: there was an art to keeping the temperatures just right, cooking long enough but not too long, stirring properly, straining and storing in a timely fashion so the lard would last until next winter's hog killing without going rancid.

Reputations were built and destroyed on less important matters.

Now, in case you don't know (although you may not want to), here's how it's done. Chunks of fat, about an inch square, are placed in a big stew pot on top of the stove – or for some people, in cauldrons over a wood fire. As the pot slowly heats – slowly because you don't want to scorch the chunks – the liquid grease seeps out of the fat. That grease is put into storage containers, and once it hardens, it's known as lard. What's left behind, the crumpled solids that give up the grease and float to the top, are called cracklings – pronounced cracklins, of course.

If Mama had been nervous about moving to the farm in the first place, that day was the epitome of her uneasiness. She was especially nervous about "cooking out the lard." She had never even *seen* it done, and it was a bit of a dangerous process with all that hot grease. Somehow, it felt like one more farm-rite of passage to her, and she desperately wanted to get it right. She kept asking Daddy how she would know when it was done, and, as many times as she asked, he answered with the same five words.

"By the way it looks."

Of course, he meant how the cracklins looked, whether they had floated to the top, whether they were crispy, beginning to brown but not burnt. But he didn't say all that, he just said, "By the way it looks."

After the long while that it took to cook the masses of pig fat, Mama filled a tea cup with the hot grease, took it into Daddy's bedroom, and held the cup under his nose so he could see it.

"Here – does this look right?"

Apparently, that was just about the funniest question my daddy had ever heard, and he started laughing. That is, he tried to laugh. The slightest movement surged him into excruciating pain, and he lay there, grunting and moaning, tears of pain and stifled laughter streaming down each temple. My mother had no idea what was so funny – she had asked a perfectly serious question (she thought). It was the only time I ever saw her get mad at him. Then she started crying. "Go ahead! Go ahead! Just lie there and laugh yourself to death! Then what am I going to tell people?"

We never had another hog-killing while living on the farm, and I suspect Mama had something to do with that fact.

~September 4, 2007~

Chapter 30

"Mars" Can Be a Real Piece of Work

Some things I just flat out do not understand. Lots of things, in fact, but at least two of them concern men – American men, that is – and some of their behavior annoys the dickens out of me.

Can anybody give me one good reason why men have to be so loud? I don't mean to establish a stereotype, 'cause, truly, not all men are obnoxious that way. Case in point, my wonderful brother-in-law. It's not the only reason I think Jim is a terrific guy, mind you, and I do so appreciate his gentle manner of speech. In fact, I have to ask him to speak up so I can hear him. Jim's no wimp; he's a giant of a guy, and he obviously has no need to prove anything by yelling.

One of my pet peeves is to go out to eat and to be forced into audio-inclusion with neighboring – even not-so-close – tables where men are engaged in competitive volume. "Hear ME! I EXIST!" And it is annoyance at its hilt in a bar: the more the alcohol, the greater the volume. I don't usually pray for anyone to drink until they pass out, but sometimes it might be a blessing for the rest of us.

159

Then there's spitting. I ask you, what is more disgusting than that?

I have a favorite sandwich place on Tucson's Fourth Avenue, nothing fancy, but the sandwiches are ample and delicious and the bread bowls of soup are dandy, too. At the back of the restaurant (using the term loosely) is an outside bar, and that's where I prefer to be. In spite of the assault to nearly all the senses – loud music that I usually don't like, bouncing off the rusty metal "décor" and concrete floor, sports on silent (thank god!) TV screens, people accompanied by their sometimes overly-eager-to-greet-and-please dogs, young women with second-skin jeans barely high enough on their hips to cover "possible" (as Grandma used to call "it"), and tattooed men and boys on alcohol and volume overload – I used to go there once every week or two, regardless of all that, to have my favorite sandwich and to read. A practice in focus, if nothing else.

I was there one afternoon, perched at a tall table, minding my own business, when I heard a different but recognizable sound. I looked up as a guy at the bar coughed, spun around and let a huge honker fly to the cement floor between the two of us. My glare nearly knocked him off his stool. He looked at me and then at where, stuck to the floor, was his contribution of poor manners, bad taste, and risk to everyone's health, and he immediately tried to make it disappear by smearing it with his shoe. I read his lips: "I'm sorry. ..."

I motioned for my server. If the guy read my lips, he saw me say, "Could you please get someone to clean the floor?" and pointing at him, adding, "That ass-hole just SPIT on it!" She rushed back with a bottle of blue-something and an armload of paper towels and cleaned it herself. He mouthed, "I'm sorry" to her and to me again, "Sorry." Maybe he was. But I bet he'll do it again, without even thinking.

My theory is that men spit like male dogs hoist their legs. If there weren't a law against it (I assume there is, I hope there is), I think men – many men – would pee on everything. Instead, they spit. Guys in sports say, "Stuff comes up and you just gotta to get rid of it!"

Swallow it, boys. I suspect you'll swallow much worse before all's said and done.

~March 13, 2009~

Chapter 31

Bag Lady in Training

O would some power the giftie gie us
to see ourselves as others see us.

~ Robert Burns, from *To a Louse, On Seeing One
on a Lady's Bonnet at Church, verse 8*

I've been thinking about change.

My niece Hannah was downright resistant to
change until she was a teenager. She finally came
to the conclusion that, paradoxically, change is here
to stay, but for years she would freak out even if her
mother wanted to buy her a new bedspread. My cat,
Boxer, didn't cotton at all to the last critter-change
in our household, that of a second cat being brought
into it. He had been the perfect gentleman-cat in
the past when another cat was adopted, and even
when dogs visited, but not so with Tess. That meant
Tess had to be given her own room – my library
– and that was a change that I found less than
acceptable. Rodney King would have said, "[Cats],
I just want to say, you know, can we all get along?
Can we get along? Can we stop making it, making

it horrible for the older [person]? ...Please, can we get along here? ...I mean, we're all stuck here for a while. ..." But I've learned that "getting along" is a change that some cats, and some people, just refuse to accept.

Tucson now has a number of red-light cameras. From what we citizenry hear, the cameras have cut down on red-light runners – at those intersections at least – and Tucson drivers and pedestrians have suffered from more than our share of those careless creeps in the past. I am thrilled that the number of accidents and fatalities are fewer, and I guess that has to mean that I am glad that those corners have changed by having cameras added; at the same time, I am not glad that the change makes Big Brother bigger.

Speaking of government, as I write this, Iran is in turmoil. Some seeking change, some voting to maintain status quo, their country is in chaos and thousands – perhaps a million – of their citizens have taken to the streets and are now being jailed or beaten or killed because they won't stop speaking up – "speaking silently" for days – about their desire for change, for more freedom. All because they feel the election was stolen from them, that it was rigged.

Where were we in America when our 2000 and 2004 elections were rigged and stolen? Were we in the streets like the Iranians? No. Had we become so complacent and spoiled that we just took every-thing, including our freedoms, for granted? Appar-ently. Because when George W. Bush, Dick Cheney, and all the other Big Brothers began to whittle away

at those freedoms – from the voting booth on – perhaps at most we sat and watched, if we paid any attention at all. Oh, there were a few people, a few in
the field of so-called journalism – a profession that
has itself morphed from news to faux-entertain-
ment – and a few on the Internet who individually
blogged or Huffington Post-ed some truth to us;
some of us nearly burned out our computers, passing
the word by email, mostly ranting to our own choirs.
Enough so that come the 2008 elections, more of us
stood up, if not in the streets, and we saw a change
that no one my age had dreamed of living to see.
My bedspread-devoted niece, at fourteen, went out
to register voters and worked for the Barack Obama
campaign, "A Change We Can Believe In." I think
that at fourteen I barely knew who was President –
little more than that folks called him "Ike."

During all these years that we have not paid enough
attention to know to be afraid of Big Brother,
we have become more afraid of our neighbors, of
strangers on the street, of other every-day human
beings, especially if we see them as "different." And
life has changed.

A while back, I went to Safeway supermarket late
one night. I was always careful to remind myself to
be alert when moving from and to my car, which
I tried to park as near to the store as possible and,
at night, in as much light as possible. Sure enough,
when I came out and started to put my groceries
into the back of my RAV4, a man started toward me
from the darkness out in front of the car. An immediate curiosity concerning safety surged through me.

165

I felt certain that such a person was going to ask for money, and I began to wonder how I would respond. His story was that the busses were no longer running, he needed a taxi to get home, he had twenty dollars worth of McDonald's cards (whatever that meant) that he'd be glad to give me in exchange for some cab money. Checking my money where he could not see me, I had only two singles and a few twenties. I wasn't that generous, so I handed him two ones, told him to keep his McDonald stuff, and he went on his way to another customer parked nearby who answered him before he got his question out: "I don't have any extra money!" I have mixed feelings about handing money over to people that way, so I just take it on a case by case basis and go by my gut, sometimes thinking it's really a scam, other times thinking, "That could be me."

I must admit, I do find the approach of strangers, especially strange-seeming strangers, and especially after dark, a wee bit scary. One night a long time ago, I was the one scaring others.

I was working for The McCall Pattern Company at the time as an educational representative. The work took me into high schools in the Midwest, but during the summers and school holidays, all the reps were housed in hotels in New York City. Daily, we reported to the tenth floor of 230 Park Avenue, a beautiful thirty-five-story structure that, although it later became known as the Helmsley Building, started out in 1929 as the headquarters of the New York Central Railroad Company. From a distance north on Park, the glory of 230's architecture dissolved against the backdrop of the larger and wider Pan Am Building (now known as The MetLife Building), but up close its unusual features could be appreciated. Three things about it always fascinated me, not the least of which was that the old queen straddled the street. The foundation floor was tunneled in a way to let the north- and southbound lanes of Park Avenue traffic pass through. It sparkles in sunlight now, but back then the pyramid-shaped roof, topped with a cupola, was green with the patina from years of air pollution having oxidized the copper. And the lobby! Ah! That lobby! I felt "so New York" whenever I entered – such elegance! The walls and floor of white travertine and glistening marble echoed the clipped steps of women's heels and men's leather soles as everyone rushed to work or ran through on their way to their offices in the upper stories or through the building on their way to Grand Central Station, which sat beyond the Pan Am building. Chinese red elevator doors with shiny brass inlays opened onto roomy cars. Every morning I stepped into one, pressed "UP," leaned against dark walls of exotic wood, and looked up at the painted clouds on the ceilings. This was my New York!

The tenth floor was a different story. The street-level lavishness did not make it up that far. Granted, time and memory may have polished the lobby's marble and brass and dulled the tenth-floor offices in my mind. As far as I know, nothing ever happened on our floor so bad as the murder some thirty-five years earlier down on the ninth when "Lucky" Luciano and Vito Genovese and two of their thick-knuckled pals had murdered their boss-of-bosses, Salvatore

Maranzano. No need to explain the line of work these men were in. However, people who worked for our boss might have understood Lucky and Vito. She was a tyrant. Again, maybe that is an exaggeration, or at the very least unfair. Maybe she was just a New York female executive of her day, and I simply a naïve bumpkin from Down South. I hate to judge. My preacher-uncle says that while the Bible says, "Judge not, that ye be not judged," it does give us license to be fruit inspectors: "By their fruits ye shall know them." By my inspection, I say Mrs. Ryan's fruits were tyrannical: she ran the place like a sweatshop.

The weeks that we reps were in the New York office, we were sewing. The outfits we wore into the schools were tailored – and I mean tailored – from a McCall's pattern. Mrs. Ryan picked the pattern (always a dress with a jacket), she picked the fabric, she picked the color. Each of us tailored two of the same outfit for ourselves for winter, two of another for summer; we were always in one while the other was at the cleaners. In the Park Avenue office for the full summer, when we finished tailoring our own "uniforms," we tailored doll clothes.

I will explain. There were five reps that went into high schools and colleges around the country, including one in Canada; there were probably about three dozen local reps who worked schools just in their hometowns. Whereas we used ourselves and a wardrobe of garments that we hauled around with us, all displayed on fancy chrome hanger-contraptions that sported fake breasts, the local reps used miniature manikins, about two feet tall. Had I been one of those women I would have felt compelled to learn ventriloquism.

Those little gals had to have clothes, too, and all the "wardrobes," which were used to teach the elements and principles of design in clothing and to brain-wash the students into buying McCall's patterns rather than, say, Simplicity or Butterick, consisted of at least a dozen garments, sometimes more. The full-time office "girls" (girls: we're talking 1968 language) constructed the majority of these little outfits, but they saved a lot of the "finger work" for us to do when we came into the city. You do the math: if there were three dozen local reps and each had to have at least a dozen little garments, that's four hundred thirty-two outfits – *per season*, mind you. They had to be hemmed. They had to have buttons. If the pattern called for bound button-holes, we made bound buttonholes – unlike regular buttonholes, they are the ones that show no thread at all and look like stubbornly clenched rectangular lips made of fabric; they are a royal pain to make in real size, and in miniature mannequin size they were maddening. In the '50s and '60s they were the rage and considered the hallmark of a well-made garment; now only fine designers use them.

There were snaps. Three thousand four hundred fifty-six snaps, to be close to precise. But snaps come in a set, a top and a bottom, so that means three thousand four hundred fifty-six times two. All the garments were slit down the back and had eight sets of snaps so the reps could be quick-change artists with their little women. Those wooden models were expensive, so McCall's sprang for only two per rep; while they were in the midst of their design spiel about one garment, they were ripping the glad-rags off and redressing the other wee one. Multitasking. Oh, yes – the miniature mannequins were never naked: they wore handmade muslin slips.

Speaking of slips. ... Our presentation was designed for home economics classrooms, but occasionally a school insisted on making our visit a full-school, auditorium event, in which case they were instructed to provide us with a clip-on mic. Not one on a stand, not a hand-held: we had to move around a lot between a table full of accessories and the rack holding the wardrobe. This wasn't just a speech; it was a performance. We were all required to give the same basic presentation, but each of us – I assume – found a way to make it our own. I quickly devised a way to test my audience, to find out how receptive they were going to be, to "connect" with them, whether there were eight or eight hundred people in front of me. That "uniform" I mentioned? Made of a forest green silk and wool blend that winter, under the waist-length jacket was an A-line dress with cap sleeves and a high neckline; I wore a gold, fleur-de-lis pin center-front on my chest. After being introduced to the audience, I began my Ryan-approved propaganda, all the while rearranging a few accessories on the table. Still yapping, I unbuttoned and removed my jacket and hung it on the wardrobe rack. Then I released the clasp on the fleur-de-lis, looked at the table as I found a place to lay it. Then: look at audience. Pause. Raise eyebrows slightly, almost apologetically. Say, "Don't worry – that's all I'm taking off!" Timing is everything, no matter how corny, and the bit never failed to serve its purpose: if they laughed, I at least knew they were listening; their expressions behind the laughter indicated just how much they were "with me." From there, I sailed.

I never have enjoyed early rises, so while traveling I had also developed a morning system that allowed me to stay in bed as long as possible. The wardrobe clothes were packed the night before, without folding the cases shut; the accessory case and handouts were carefully sorted and packed. Everything ready for a quick get-away. After the second clock alarmed, followed by the downstairs desk calling to get me finally out of bed, it was brush teeth, shower, put on bra and non-cling half-slip. Do the make-up thing. Call downstairs for bellman to call cab and come up to get the three bags I had to tote to every school. Put on dress. Once bellman arrives, don jacket – and sometimes, hat.

One morning in Little Rock, Arkansas I went through the preparation that had served me perfectly for months, but that morning there were some glitches. I had just started to put my dress on when there was a knock on the door. I had hardly put the receiver back in its cradle, and the bellman was already there, interrupting my morning rhythm. A bigger glitch awaited me at the school: the principal was for some reason impressed that anyone from New York City was coming to his school, and he wanted to make it a huge show. This was Little Rock's Central High School, famous – or infamous

– for its role in integration some years earlier. The auditorium was filled with eight hundred students – including boys, for whom the program should hold absolutely no interest; stage right was cornered with an arc of about ten chairs to provide seating for faculty and staff of what importance I couldn't tell and including a minister who, first up, blessed the whole affair.

There was a rack for the wardrobe, a table for the accessories – and a stand-up mic. I explained to the home economics teacher, my actual host, that this was not going to work, that I could not carry the mic because I needed both my hands for the presentation. She selected a student as sweet as her name to follow along behind me while holding the microphone in front of me, and I began my audience test, as usual: I talked, Cherry held the mic perfectly. Then I removed my jacket. At that moment I felt a cold breeze on my bare back: my dress, which had a zipper from the neckline to the bottom of my butt was wide open, and the only thing keeping me from stripping on stage was a tiny hook and eye at the neckline. I casually – well, as casually as sudden panic allows – turned my head away from the mic and whispered around my back to Cherry, "Can you zip me up without anyone seeing? I'll hold the mic." The hand off, the zip-up, the return of the mic – it was smooth, it was inconspicuous, it was perfect! I don't know whether it was sheer relief or the image that kept popping into my mind – me, standing on stage in a navy blue half-slip and bra, a pile of forest green fabric around my ankles, eight hundred people looking on, four hundred of them being teenage boys – whatever the reason, I chuckled throughout the entire presentation.

But I digress. It's easy to do when remembering The McCall Pattern Company and Mrs. Ryan. The memories alone can make my eyes glaze over and strange air sounds pass through my lips. We worked in the office for eight hours and then took bags full of those little outfits back to our hotel rooms, work totaling ten to twelve hours a day. One week – this is burned into my memory – I sewed on eleven hundred little bitty hooks and eyes. Did I say sweat-shop? Did I say stooped shoulders? Sore fingers? Teary eyes? Did I mention hit-man thoughts?

And back to a Friday in the office when we had all been tailoring our own outfits. ... Mrs. Ryan was to inspect our work on Monday; it was Friday and I was not quite finished and I did not have a sewing machine in my room at the hotel. One of the regulars in the office invited me to go to her apartment after work and use her machine. Janice lived nearby, east of Lexington, I think maybe on Forty-third Street. Each of us sewed and pressed seams until about eleven o'clock that night, and I had to stop, pack up my goodies, and go home. I left her build-ing only to realize that the doorman was off duty by then and there were no cabs cruising the street. No choice but to begin the walk to my hotel, about seven mostly dark, New York blocks away.

Fortunately, I wasn't particularly afraid because of something I had learned soon after being hired. A local rep from Miami was in training at the same time as I. We connected quickly and palled around together for the short time she was in the city. Nei-ther of us had ever been to New York and we were a bit terrified of the possibility of getting mugged or raped or murdered – never really deciding which option might be the worst. Then, somehow, we found out that that particular year, Charlotte, North Carolina – my own neck-of-the-woods – was boasting the highest crime rate in the country, and Miami was claiming the second highest. New York City was something like twelfth, for heaven's sake! We strutted fearlessly after that. Not carelessly, but fearlessly.

So, that memorable Friday night, I left Janice's apartment and began my mid-night trek, eyes wide open, but not afraid. By the time I had covered half of my seven blocks back to the Roosevelt, I was laughing – laughing at the absurdity of human nature, assumptions, fear. As soon as I turned the corner onto Lexington Avenue, I was astonished at how many people were on the streets, mostly well dressed, dating couples mainly, some single stragglers. Then I began to notice everyone crossing to the other side of the street, to stroll, to window shop, glancing my way, and I wondered what I was missing. What I was missing was what they had been seeing, what had prompted them to cross the street – rather, what they thought they had been seeing as they had been approaching me.

Leaving Janice's, I had packed my heavy sewing into a brown paper shopping bag that I carried in my left hand, along with a flashlight she had let me borrow. My iron had been too hot to put in with the clothes, so I carried it in my other hand, out in front of me. Every step I took blasted a shot of steam out of the iron, along with a loud whoosh. I steam-cleaned Lexington Avenue as well as Forty-Fifth Street, all the way back to the hotel. My side of the streets, anyway: people crossed over in droves at the sight of me. Their assumptions changed me from a sweat-shop victim into a full-fledged, cackling bag lady, barreling down the streets of Manhattan.

~June 22, 2009~

Chapter 32

Lightered Knots and Lash LaRue

There are a few things for which I'm not sure I have ever forgiven my daddy. Now, enough time has passed that it really doesn't matter, but time healing wounds is not exactly the same as forgiving. Years become a greater gift when they include appropriately timed forgiveness, and the gift is of larger measure for the forgiver than for the forgiven.

The man never threw a thing away in his whole life, or so it seemed, and I suppose that's how I came by that tendency so honestly. He'd just build another shed or lean-to by another one down behind the house and stash stuff, even cardboard boxes and strings of twine – not balls of twine, mind you, *strings* of twine. However, something came over him once when I was away at college, and he decided to go up into the attic and do a little "cleaning out." I never could tell if there was more room up there after that, but I did realize something was missing. What was missing was my more-than-two-foot-high stack of comic books.

When I was a kid in the '40s and early '50s I wasn't granted many requests during shopping trips, but, whenever I asked for one, my mother would usually give me a dime for a "funny book," as they were called then, even if humorless. Reading was important to her, and I suppose she wanted me to read anything that I wanted to read.

We were living in Sanford before I started to school, and Mama would have me crawl into bed with her every night for her to read me a story. My very favorite nights were when she would read from "Uncle Remus." I was in love with that old storyteller.

In years since, quite a fuss has been made over Joel Chandler Harris's stories being racist. I've never been one to agree with that, but then I'm not Black and, if I were, perhaps I'd think differently about it. I never remember reading anything at all that Harris himself said that was racist. Uncle Remus, his wise old character, referred to the Negroes of the post-Civil War South by names that are today anything but "politically correct." I might be way off base here, and if I took time to read the Uncle Remus tome that rests in my library today, I might find much more to be embarrassed about than I am remembering. I'm sure there are plenty of people who will take issue even with my saying "Black" and "Negro" instead of "African American." But these stories, and the old man Uncle Remus, were born way back in 1879, and while the narrator – Harris – used respectful language, it was Uncle Remus, an old post-war black man himself, who used monikers, the likes of which get people like Don Imus fired today.

Harris was a young editor at "The Atlanta Constitution" and his stories revealed not only Black culture, but Southern society in general, with all the warts and roses. Some folks today, "fokes," Uncle Remus would say, complain vehemently about the way the stories were written, that is, in the Black vernacular of the time. That NEVER struck me as being racist, either, because, for the most part, Uncle Remus sounded like he could have been kin to me. Why, if I were writing this the way I sound, I dare say you would not have made it to this paragraph. Granted, now and then that dialect is extremely hard to read, particularly so unless one grew up hearing such sounds:

"You leave dat box right whar she is, an, let de 'oman take wun young un an you take de udder wun, an' den you git in de middle er de big road an' pull out fer de place whar you come fum. I'm preachin' now."

Uncle Remus did do that: he preached. There were morals in the stories. They taught about good and bad; they taught about hard work and fairness; they taught about love and family and friendship and loyalty and honesty. Anyway, those are the things I remember about Uncle Remus stories, and I didn't come away from them calling people inappropriate names, even though my daddy and his peers saw no wrong in doing it – and did.

There were words and things about words I heard that I didn't understand. Years later, when I was in fourth grade at Harrisburg School, I was reading Uncle Remus for myself by then, and I came across a word I had never seen: mulatto. My mother explained to me that a mulatto was someone who was

179

half black and half white.

I said, "Oh – like Miss Lucy!"

But it wasn't. Miss Lucy worked behind the food line in the school cafeteria, and every day of the school year that she scooped lunch onto my plate and handed it to me, I never failed to be fascinated by the big splashes of pinkish-white color on her otherwise dark brown arms and face. My assumption was wrong, even if logical: instead of being a mulatto, she must have had vitiligo, now thought probably to be an autoimmune disease.

Other Uncle Remus words I didn't understand until many years later. Some of what he had to say came to be considered proverbs; one of them was "Moon may shine, but a lightered knot's mighty handy."

In 1970 I moved from Elizabeth City to pursue an art education degree at Pembroke State College (as it was called then) while living with my close friend Ellen outside Lumberton, North Carolina. Almost immediately, Ellen and I started remodeling the 125-year-old house that had belonged to her grandparents. We tore out the ramshackle six-foot windows in the bedroom we were working on. The empty rectangles that remained had to be made shorter and wider in preparation for the two modern windows she had bought for the room. I could skip mentioning our stupidity, but I won't. Mind you, we had never done any remodeling before this, but when Ellen couldn't find any carpenter who was willing to take on such a "small" project (hardly how we described it at the end of the summer), I said,

"Ellen, we can read, we can do it!" I sounded like the DIY channel before it existed. So I went to the lumberyard and bought a dollar-ninety-eight book on carpentry. It was sufficiently informative, regardless of what you may be thinking, and we actually did a fine job, if I say so myself. But the stupid thing was that we bought the windows, measured one for one of the openings, painstakingly and proudly prepared the space, and when we got ready to install the thing, we hadn't left any room at all for "play" – one would have had to hold the window outside, perfectly parallel to the wall of the house, and slide it straight into the hole; there was no room to arc it in. We had to cut out what we had added to the top of the opening to make the old hole small enough – yeah, small enough – and start all over. Well, not everything we needed to know was in that dollar-ninety-eight book, including common sense.

Except for that mistake, the shortening was easy; the widening of the opening was a different story. Ellen ruined two blades and nearly burned out the circular saw motor trying to cut through the six-by-eight upright frame on the side of the old window. Those old houses were built like forts in terms of the structural forms – and without a single nail, all wooden pegs – yet the cypress floorboards were separated by half-inch cracks that allowed us to peer down to the raw underside of the house and let the cold of winters sift up to the only bed in the house until we finished the remodeling. Old timers believed a house needed to "breathe." The folks who allowed this means of "breathing" never needed a dustpan. We had spent our first winter there with roofing tar paper on the floor and little squares of carpet samples that trailed into the room from the doorway to each side of the bed, like colorful stepping stones in a garden – a "garden" with twelve-foot ceilings, six-foot windows with broken panes, and enough insecurity to cause Ellen to feel the necessity of sleeping with a pistol under her pillow. She may have felt more secure, but I can't say the same for myself.

But back to that upright by the window: the reason it was so hard is that it was "fat-lightered," and that's when and where I learned what Uncle Remus had meant by "a lightered knot." Pine is amply embedded with resin – some pieces more than others – and when the resin hardens, which it does over time, especially after one hundred and twenty-five years, it's almost as hard as petrified wood, and not at all friendly toward a Skilsaw blade or the person using it. It's dangerous, in fact. Every time Ellen would try to start cutting through the thick stud, that sucker kicked the saw back like a .12-gauge shotgun after a blast. It's when the resin hardens that it's called "fat lighter," and if that house had ever caught fire it would've gone to ashes in five minutes, no doubt, just like a bundle of kindling or a cheap trailer.

I recently read of a house fire in Dothan, Alabama. The fire chief said, "You can't put out these old fat lighter houses, I don't care how much water you use." Then there was the church that burned to a crisp in Georgia last month. The preacher said that the church was one hundred years old and "made of heart pine, and as everyone knows," he said, "fat lighter wood is highly flammable." Sure, everyone knows that. He also 'lowed as how the devil didn't like some of the good things that had been happening in that church, such as his own teachings on "Why Evolution Isn't Right." Well, somebody ought to explain to him that the heart pine had evolved into one hell of a fire propellant over the last hundred years.

All that just goes to show there is simply no better kindling for a fire or a fireplace than fat lighter. And that is why Uncle Remus reminded folks that moonlight might be helpful, but a burning piece of fat-lightered pine would make a really good light. Plus, it smells of a mighty fine aroma.

Actually, reading Uncle Remus dialect is pretty hard work, and few of the stories are short. So, usually, the stories Mama read to me before bedtime during those pre-school nights in Sanford came from *Little Golden Books*. Before 1942, children's books cost about two dollars each, a lot of money for most people back then. But someone got the bright idea to make small, inexpensive ones that would sell for twenty-five cents and appeal to a lot of people, and the first dozen titles of *Little Golden Books* began to be born, two months before I was. Mama gave voice to adventures that transported me into the worlds of "The Little Red Hen" or "Dumbo" or "The Lively Little Rabbit" or "The Puppy That Grew and Grew and Grew." Of course, none of these books held truly believable stories, but I thought the puppy one really was a bit too much: by the time he had grown to be bigger than the circus tent, I think that, even at that young age, I felt the writer had insulted me. One night I crawled into Mama's bed with *The Little Golden Book* I had selected, "The Saggy, Baggy Elephant," and announced that I was going to read to her. To her astonishment and thrill, I read the entire book with no mistakes. She didn't know I could read at all. What followed were trips to the library and the beginning of my collection of comic books.

I read a lot of them. The fledgling genre of super-heroes didn't appeal to me except for Superman now and then and always Plastic Man; I thought it was so funny – and convenient – how he could reach around corners or over houses or stretch himself to Kingdom Come. I liked that even better than Superman's soaring powers. But first and foremost, I preferred Westerns. I read about the Lone Ranger and Tonto, Roy Rogers and Dale Evans, Gene Autry, Hopalong Cassidy, Red Ryder, Silvertip, and Lash LaRue, who had the greatest name of all.

Soon, favorites were formed among the artists that had made these pages come to life for me and for thousands of other kids – mostly boys, I would imagine. That's how I learned to draw: I especially loved the way Silvertip comics were drawn, and I liked the Lone Ranger drawings. Some of the others, the Roy Rogers ones in particular, were too fine-lined and wimpy. I was totally fascinated by the thick and thin of the lines that somebody had known how to put on paper to create the expression on Silvertip's face, and that somebody else had known how to draw the curl of the Masked Man's upper lip whenever he came face to face with the bad guy. The India ink shadows and every *BANG!* and *BLAM!* and *OWW!* provided hours of observation, long after the storyline had ended. I sat and looked at my favorite frames and drew, matching to the best of my young ability, the curve, the angle, the thick and the thin, and wishing I had a pencil that could make darker lines and shadows than my standard No. 2 pencil could do.

There is no rhyme or reason, in my mind, as to what possessed Daddy to throw away my precious stack of comics – my preserved favorites, the culled best of all I had ever had, pages that had mentored me and "taught" me to draw – why he decided, of all the stuff in the attic – let alone in all those sheds – to throw them out. When I discovered the loss years after he had burned them in the trash barrel behind the pump house, he said he was sorry but he didn't think I would still want them, they were "just old funny books." I told him he had set fire to what might amount to a couple thousand dollars. I think that is what stirred his regret.

As I said, I don't think I ever really forgave him, but by now it doesn't matter that they are gone; and if I had them, I probably still wouldn't want to trade them for money, and they'd just be further cluttering up my house. Or sheds. I may not have the comics, but I still have a few of those early drawings in a smelly, old red scrapbook that Mama saved. And now, almost sixty years later, some of my paintings carry the influence of that early love of the Western comic book – and I at last have access to a really rich black for the lines and the shadows.

One more remnant of that early love affair: to this day – and I know this sounds crazy, but it can be fun in otherwise boring situations – sometimes when people are speaking to me, I "see" text bubbles over their heads, just like they are drawn in the funny books. I "move" the bubbles around, changing the little dangling, curved pointers appropriately, so as to make a better composition with whatever else is in "the frame."

It really is quite entertaining. Try it sometime – especially in an otherwise boring crowd.

~August 22, 2007~

Chapter 33

My Sister's a Call Girl

At age twenty-four I found myself in the Big Apple.

I'm not sure just what it was that possessed me to think I should be there. I was a college graduate, I had taught home economics for two years, which included teaching sewing, and I wasn't fully stupid, but I was shy – and far from sophisticated. I had never been to New York City. Why, I doubt that by then I had ever even seen a color television screen. I suppose the same naiveté that failed to inform me not to drive from North Carolina to 230 Park Avenue prompted me to say yes when I was offered the job I had applied for, not to mention how I was swayed by the impressive and grand old building that housed the offices. A few weeks later, when I flew to New York to begin the training program, it was my first time on an airplane.

I began working for The McCall Pattern Company as an Educational Representative, a job that for two years I first enjoyed, eventually tolerated, and finally hated. There were three Ed-Reps, as we were called, who traveled three vertical bands of the United States visiting high schools, plus one who visited colleges throughout the country, and two more in Canada who attended to both education levels. Our job was "soft-sell" – teaching the elements and principles of design in regard to clothing and style during a single class period filled with sewing students. We hoped that as soon as we left town, they would rush to their nearest retailer and buy McCall's patterns instead of the Simplicity or Butterick or Advance brands. Simplicity had their own "girls" competing with similar efforts.

Having grown up on a farm, then living in small towns, I was accustomed to familiarity in my ears – cows lowing, chickens clucking and crowing, tractors whirring in the fields, Canada geese that honked their way every year to the ponds and watering holes, the occasional traffic passing by the house, and then the usual town-sounds that one eased into naturally and that spelled out the lives of neighbors and busy shoppers. New York City was a cacophony blazing through my senses. The sounds overwhelmed me; there were times that they seemed so alive, so heavy, that I felt I would suffocate. Visually, I was enthralled by the variety, but there were times that I felt claustrophobic on the streets and walked with my eyes turned upward, keeping watch on the imagined outlet that was a sliver of sky. Emotionally, I think I was lonely. Looking back so many years later, it almost seems like the entire time spent there was like living an out-of-body experience. Odd, but one thing I remember loving was standing on a corner waiting for a light to change and smelling bus exhaust. Is that sick, or what?

While the other young women in the office, some new like me, some "veterans," were quite likeable, as was Janice, our immediate trainer, the head of the Pattern Division was a terror. I don't remember ever seeing Mrs. Ryan smile. She was a growl made flesh. In stature and style she had sort of a Betty Friedan-look about her, which is probably why I never could read Friedan's books, but, I can assure you, I don't think Mrs. Ryan had a feminist bone in her body. She was made completely of rules, results, and rudeness.

She instructed Janice to write the program that we were to present during the next months to thousands of students and teachers. In our respective hotel rooms where McCall's housed us when in the city, we each read and reread page after page after page – thirty-some, if I remember correctly – preparing to memorize the presentation our trainer had penned and which we would practice in front of each other and Janice – and eventually Mrs. Ryan – in the Park Avenue tenth floor offices. Rote learning is not my bag. Never has been. That summer in New York I spent more time pacing and crying than learning. I kept trying but I could not do it. There I was, in The Big City, in Big Business, among Big People (I perceived), not belonging, wondering what in the world I was doing there, not knowing who I was. If I was expected to be someone else, even in speech – well, it was crazy-making! Finally, something inside me said: I have to do this in my own voice, not someone else's. When I offered the suggestion to the trainer, bless her, she agreed to let me try and, while it still wasn't easy with little time left before hitting the road, I did it, and I did it to applause. (It was simply their expression of relief, surely.) Soon, August and the school year were upon us and we all set out for our final training in actual schools, taking turns with classes for a week in the sweet rolling countryside of Carlisle, Pennsylvania. After that, we were on our own, and I embarked on my lone assignment, eager to get the northernmost schools covered before winter fell with its Upper Midwest fury.

That first year, my territory stretched from Milwaukee to San Antonio, from Omaha to Memphis, and included other cities in eleven states. The nitty-gritty of the job involved flying to a different city each week (one a week usually, two or more weeks in larger cities with multiple suburbs, such as five weeks around Kansas City), checking into a hotel, asking about a decent restaurant or two, unpacking the bags, and settling in to telephone the teachers with whom I'd be spending the week. The luggage consisted of two monstrous green wardrobe cases of hanging clothes. The swivel loop of the hanger continued down to form a trapezoid shape of heavy chrome wire, and inside this area were extra wire appendages, elongated ovals reaching from the sides toward the center, and around which tissue paper was wrapped, effecting symbolic teenage breasts and filling out the garments. The clothes were made from our patterns selected by Mrs. Ryan and others in the hopes that they would appeal to everyone within earshot of our Gospel of Style according to McCall's.

Besides the wardrobe cases, there was other luggage,

too: another case of accessories and McCall's commercial propaganda to hand out to the students and teachers, two personal bags, and my baritone ukulele case. That uke was good company: except for the time in a few cities, I wasn't much of a "party girl" – and I may have to think twice before sharing some of those stories. ...

We tailored our own clothes while in New York, made from our patterns, of course, and traveled with two identical outfits to accommodate dry cleaning time. We used ourselves as models, using the accessory collection to teach scale. If we were in one school all day, we delivered our spiel four times; if we had been scheduled to go to two schools, we spoke once in one school and twice in the other, and in all the classes, each hanger was lifted off and back onto a clothes rack at least once. Back at the hotel every day these two-dozen garments had to be removed from the wardrobe cases and hung on a rack in the hotel room. Within a week's time I'm sure I handled enough heavy chrome to make an Edsel bumper. In no time flat, I was so accustomed to the presentation that I could've pulled an ear and it would've spilled out of me, so I found ways to test my audience's attention and sense of humor, play with them, and keep each presentation interesting not only for them but, frankly, mainly for me.

The second year I switched territories; I was given the entire East Coast, and schedules would include most but not all of those twenty-three states. Until then, I had been in primarily upper middle class schools. In other words, White. Even though integration was by then the law of the land, I was now visiting schools that were all Black. I was delivering my carefully honed message to tops of heads on a number of days: heads on folded arms collapsed on the classroom tables, heads of students who slept through their classes because it was the only time they had to sleep. Their teachers would explain to me that most of them came from a one-parent home and that most often the mother had to be at home with younger children during the day and work nights, so these young girls, being deprived of their education by desperately needed sleep, had been the ones at home taking care of the crying or sick babies at night. Or the alternate scenario: some of these children had to work a job all night in order to help provide for their family, so they would leave work, come to school, and sleep. Every teacher would tell me this, and every one of them would say, "Please – don't take it personally."

In spite of ending on a very sour note with Mrs. Ryan, there are some fond memories I have of working for The McCall Pattern Company. It was a great opportunity to see the country – although the pay was crap: a hundred dollars a week, if you can believe that! I had a chance to consider some places I might like to live, and I met some great people. There was a history teacher in Little Rock whom I met in the teacher's lounge during a break. She asked me if I had seen their beautiful city.

I said, "Well, from the windows of cabs between the hotel and schools."

She clapped her hands together and said, "I'll pick

you up Saturday at nine!"

She took me on a tour of the city for the entire day, her itinerary based not on architecture or parks or homes, but rather on trees she had discovered that she found fascinating. I only remember that one looked like a woman in a wedding gown, one looked like a bear. How could I forget that woman? She shared one of the most creative ideas I've ever heard of!

My boyfriend at the time, whom I almost-married-but-didn't-thank-god, came to New York to visit me once during all the time I worked for The McCall Pattern Company. A red neon light somewhere outside my hotel flashed a red light into my room every night. It never bothered me in the least except when he was sleeping beside me. At the same time, I was involved with my first girlfriend. She came to visit when I was working in New Orleans and at least three times to New York. Those were wonderful visits – except for the disastrous final time, when she unexpectedly brought her new girlfriend with her, left abruptly early without looking back, and without so much as a "goodbye."

Right now, I'm not remembering which city I was in, but I was staying at a Holiday Inn. On Saturday, I went out to sit by the pool and read. Quite a few guys were there, having a great time in a well-behaved way, and they all seemed to be acquainted with each other. One came over, introduced himself as Keith, sat beside me, tried to get me to go swimming, but we just talked instead. After a bit, I asked if they were all together. He said yes, that they all belonged to a band whose name I didn't recognize, not being much of a rock and roll fan. He started pointing to each one and introducing them: "... and that last guy with the big lips is Mick Jagger." I had no idea I was supposed to be impressed. My informant was Keith Richards.

Speaking of musicians, the only almost-affair I had while traveling was with a drummer in Tulsa. He was handsome as the dickens and played with a pretty good band in my hotel. One of these days I should dig out their old album and see what his name was. We spent a lot of time together after his gigs while I was there; it went as far as I wanted but I can't say the same for him.

So, in that regard at least, I remained a "good girl" on the road, in spite of the fact that Lori, my little sister who was six then and couldn't remember the complete name of the company I worked for, told everybody her sister was a "'Call girl in New York City."

~August 30, 2008~

Chapter 34

Half Past Midnight, July

The '60s in America: hippies, Woodstock, drugs, Beatles, Motown, and the Vietnam War. The '60s in America: maimed veterans back home and ignored; assassinations; violent differences between "hawks" and "doves" while racial tensions teemed in the South, in the North, and on both coasts. The '60s in America: a time when on one sunny day in 1967, while hippies loved and Elvis sang, someone gave me a cab ride through a small corner of hell, a free ride of great price.

After living in northeastern North Carolina during my first two years out of college, I moved to New York City in June of 1966 to work as an Educational Representative for The McCall Pattern Company. It was a job that paid almost nothing – only a hundred dollars a week. What it lacked in salary was made up for in travel to cities within thirty-three states.

My first school year as an ed-rep had me taking The McCall Pattern Company's propaganda into our Midwestern territory: from Minneapolis to San Anton', Omaha to Memphis, and dozens of cities between. I had become comfortable with my presentations in the high school classrooms and auditoriums, the majority of which had been filled with middle- to upper-middle-class white students. The students and teachers were polite, attentive, and they were impressed with the program that McCall's was providing.

Fourteen months into the job, I began promoting the advantages of buying McCall's patterns in a whole battery of new cities: my territory had been shifted from that vertical ribbon in the middle of the country to states east of the Mississippi. I wasn't sure what to expect, but I did know that many of the schools would likely bear little or no similarity to the ones I had visited the year before. Sure enough, my first assignment for the '67-'68 school year was two weeks in the Detroit school system.

The hotel bellboy carried my bags out to a cab on my first Monday in Detroit. The driver was a humorless sort, but that was fine with me that time of morning; I wasn't interested in conversation. We arrived at a school suggestive of a prison without fencing. Even in the sweltering summer heat, it emitted a chill like a medieval castle. It was a massive square building on a bit of a hill, with expansive lawns all around it, and stripes of unending sidewalks from the streets up to doors centered on each facade. The cab driver retrieved the bags from the trunk and set them on the walk; he stood there and stared at the building, the bags, and me.

"Not safe to leave these bags unattended," he said. "Don't let them out of your sight."

Knowing I couldn't carry them all at once myself, he helped me get them to the classroom. His warning set the tone for my two weeks in Detroit.

Remember – the year before I had been in primarily upper-middle-class schools. In other words, the majority of students were white. Even though integration was by then the law of the land, I was now visiting schools with all Black students. Now I would now be going into schools that were quite different. I would find them filled to the brim with students whose lives bore little resemblance to those of the others I had met. I would discover them to be mostly black, mostly poor, mostly tired and sleepy, and the majority of them could not care less that I had flown in from New York, that I was in my carefully tailored silk wool dress and jacket and felt pill box hat.

On my fourth day in Detroit, the hotel bellboy carried my bags out to a cab. My morning driver was a wiry little thing, not an ounce of waste about her. Short and tiny in stature, with pure muscle under her glistening dark skin, she moved like a gazelle from the trunk to my door to hers. I noticed how she looked at home behind the wheel, and when I gave her the address, she pulled confidently into traffic. I didn't strike up any conversation since I'm slow to wake up early in the morning, but she was curious as to why I was going so far out to a school, so I explained why I was in town, what was in the bags, and what I would be doing all day. Once we arrived at the school, she asked if I'd like for her to pick me up that afternoon. What a relief that would be! I wouldn't have to bother calling another cab and have to wait on the street for its arrival, guarding McCall's precious bags.

When I finished my work day and went to the front door, there she was, waiting for me. This school was in one of Detroit's far eastern suburbs and the drive back toward town was most pleasant, with little traffic, along wide streets with tree-lined medians, and I was awake enough to enjoy it. She and I shared some chatter about our day, about where we came from, that sort of thing.

Then she looked at me in her rear-view mirror and said, "Did you hear about the riots?"

I grew up on a farm in the Piedmont area of North Carolina. My parents were good people who were plain and hardworking. Mama's formal education ended in the seventh grade (as I remember; my sister remembers ninth), and Daddy's in the sixth. As for me, after three years of "town schooling," I attended a country school during grades four through twelve, a school so small that we had only forty-four seniors in our 1960 graduating class. I was reared in a Christian home among a horde of fundamentalist relatives and when it came time to choose a college, I admit with a cringe that I considered going to what was then the most fundamentalist college in the South – Bob Jones University in South Carolina. Thank God, after visiting that school, I instead enrolled in East Carolina College, now known as East Carolina University, in the eastern part of our state. To put it mildly, I had led a very sheltered life.

The only black people I had known were a man I dearly loved at our grocery store in town, the old man who lived down behind our property, and the Weeks family who lived as tenants on our farm. I loved Lucille and John and while our families were friendly, I didn't know their children well – Mary and Harriet were more my age but their little brother was much younger. I am sorry I cannot think of his name – that bashful little boy who spent most of his quiet childhood on our farm – who, as soon as he was old enough, left Cabarrus County to join the Army, who was sent to Vietnam, never to come home again. I lost track of the Weeks family after Daddy quit farming and turned the land into pasture. That's when they moved away. But years later when visiting Daddy, I asked him to help me find where they lived. Lucille beamed when she came to the door and saw me standing at the door with Daddy. I asked about her family and that's when she told me about her son. He was dead, she said; John, too. "His broken heart finally took him on to the Lord." One of their daughters, Harriet, grew up to be a nurse in the hospital where Mama spent her last days.

The only other "colored people" – the kinder of two references back then – with whom I had come in contact were the ones hired to pick our cotton and Mr. Stovall who lived on property behind our farm. Both of my parents worked in a hosiery mill in Concord, and Daddy was also working the farm, Mama helping every way she could. The mill owned Mama's time from seven to three and Daddy's from three to eleven. Daddy would get home a little before midnight, sleep a few hours, then get up and take the pickup into town to find workers during cotton-picking season. When I was much too young to drive a car, Daddy taught me how to drive the tractor, assemble the old iron scales onto its hydraulic lift, and weigh each picker's collection of fluff that their dry, splitting fingers had culled from the cotton bolls during the past eight or ten hours. Throughout the day, I would carry jugs of sweet iced tea and water and glasses down to the field to be sure they all had enough to drink; they would stop for a midday half hour to eat the lunch they had brought with them. Then at day's end, when Daddy was back at the mill, I would attach the scales to the old Ford tractor's hydraulic lift, weigh the giant piles of cotton, and report the number to Mama, who would multiply the weight by the meager wages-per-pound and dole the cash out to the workers. They would then climb into the bed of the pickup – I don't know how they could lift a leg by then – sit on the benches Daddy had built for them, and Mama would drive them back to their neighbor-hood shanties in Concord, me in tow.

One of those cotton pickers stands out in my mind. Although Mama never had an enemy in the world and people even called her a saint – one woman seemed to hate her; why, I didn't know. That tiny woman, who wasn't five feet tall and couldn't have weighed a hundred pounds wet, picked more cotton than anyone else in the field, more than twice her own weight, every day that she picked. (It won't really give you a clue as to just how much that is, but go into your bathroom and pull out a cotton ball. Light as a feather, no? Try to imagine how many of them it would take to weigh over two hundred pounds!) Anyway, those are two reasons I remember her, but the main reason is her name. No matter how many days she worked for us, over how many summers, she would always, every single day, announce her name to Mama who made the pay chart at weighing time. Mama knew her name, of course, but she would strut forward, stand as tall as she could stretch herself, and provide much of her history with the announcement of her name: Hattie Lucinda Ford Polk Peeler. How could I ever forget the rhythm of that? And now, so many years later, I can understand her resentment toward white privilege that I read as anger; I can understand her need, and reason, to stand proud and tall – to be Hattie Lucinda Ford Polk Peeler, in all the glory she could muster.

In our neck of the woods, talk of integration began to come up as I approached high school age.

"I'll tell you right now, no young' un of mine will ever use the same bathroom as a nigger!"

"But Daddy, what difference does it make? If we're all God's children and our only difference is in our skin color, what difference does it make if we go to school together or use the same bathroom?"

"It's just not right!" he would say.

Daddy was a mighty good man, but in this respect he was a product of his time. I could love John and Lucille all I wanted, but according to Daddy, I for sure wasn't going to pee in the same place their children did. It made no sense to me.

Any kind of connection I felt with these few people of a color unlike my own came from more of a spiritual place than a political one; it didn't occur to me that there might be any way that I, personally, could influence any kind of change for equality. I didn't even have a vocabulary for such thoughts. For a long time, I didn't know what was going on at the lunch counter in Greensboro; I didn't know what was going on in Selma; I had no idea who Martin Luther King Jr., was; I had no knowledge of Rosa Parks's bravery on a bus; I was unaware of killings and hangings and bombings that were going on in the South in those days. Truth be confessed, the first time I could vote in a Presidential election, I voted for Nixon, not Kennedy. Too much sheltering causes blindness. However, as time passed, my eyes had opened a bit on what had transpired between my childhood and that summer of 1967.

A major eye-opener had come two years before. I was driving back from Norfolk to Elizabeth City, where I was living. My girlfriend and I were enjoying the late-night cruise in my new GTO. All the windows were down, the damp smells were rushing in on the wind, and we were talking about the tiny "spy-camera" she had just bought at the Naval Base commissary. I saw a glow in the distance.

Sprawling between that lowest, outside part of Virginia and down into northeastern North Carolina is an area called the Great Dismal Swamp – an honest-to-god miserable swamp (hence its name, I suppose) that George Washington himself surveyed years ago in order for a canal to be built connecting the Chesapeake Bay and Albemarle Sound. It was begun in 1793 and for twelve backbreaking years of nasty sludge, intolerable mosquitoes, and way too many water moccasins, nearby landowners hired out their slaves to do the work, which they did almost entirely by hand. The canal is the oldest continually operating man-made canal in the United States, and it became part of the Intracoastal Waterway. Ironically, and thankfully, the canal became useful years later as a part of the Underground Railroad. A smidgen of poetic justice, perhaps.

We were about twenty miles from home, in the middle of the swamp and a night black as pitch, buzzing down the narrow two-lane pavement that runs parallel to the unseen canal and nearing one of the rare intersections that butted into that highway. There was a field-clearing on the far corner. In the field were dozens of men in white robes and hats, and in the midst of them was a twenty-foot cross, aflame. I slowed to a crawl and then a stop. Gayle leaned across me with her new Minolta to snap a picture when a man's arm came from nowhere through the window as he tried to snatch the camera from her hand. I could smell his sweaty arm as it passed my face. I couldn't believe what I was witnessing, and I had no idea what they might do to us. By then I'd heard of cross-burnings, but never, ever would I have thought I'd see one! I was just a Caucasian passing by in a car – still it was terrifying. I can't begin to imagine what a Black family felt, waking in the middle of a night to one burning on their own front lawn. A few years later, I almost married a guy from those woods, and only this minute, over four decades later, it occurs to me to wonder if he might have been in that field that night. There are times to be thankful to be sitting on top of the power of a '65 GTO and times to be thankful I didn't marry Billy of the Swamp (whether he was there that night or not). I floored the gas pedal, leaving the men and their curses and the Great Dismal Swamp behind. ...

In between my growing-up days and my arrival in Detroit, this country had been through some of its worst history. We had been mired in the Vietnam War, President Kennedy had been assassinated – followed quickly by the assassination of his assassin, and the world may never know the real truth of all that. Martin Luther King Jr. had been murdered, and two months later, Robert Kennedy. Integration was not going well, and for many reasons there were racial riots in a number of cities. In that summer of '67, Detroit was one of them, and I had read about their July riots in *Life* magazine and looked at the disturbing photos.

Furthermore, I heard some disturbing news in one of the first Detroit schools that I visited. That day, conversation in the teachers' lounge turned to the riots, and one of the teachers told me that her husband had not slept much at all since those horrendous nights weeks before. He was a firefighter and a member of the National Guard, so when the Guard was called to duty to quell the uprising, he was assigned to ride in a tank. He came home one morning and told her that the captain of the tank had ordered a car to stop, one that for some reason was suspected of containing an arsenal. After repeated orders to the four black men to stop and get out, he told his wife, they still refused to obey and the captain ordered the tank operator to roll over the car. He did. She said she felt so sorry for her husband – and for the families of those men, who surely never had a clue what became of them that night and would wonder forever why they never came home.

So, yes, by August of '67 I knew a little more of what our country was like since those days of my innocence, of shelter, of blindness, and it included some of what had transpired in Detroit only a month before I had arrived there.

The cab driver's name was Sharon, I think. I'll say it was, because I want always to remember her and I want her image that lives in my mind to have a name even if it isn't the one she told me that day. So, taking a studied look at me over her glasses and through the mirror behind her windshield, Sharon asked, "Did you hear about the riots?" and I said yes.

She said, "Do you want to see where it happened?"

Time. It took time to answer.

"Yes and no," I answered honestly. And then, "Yes."

A slight smile of understanding livened the lines of life by her eyes, and her slender fingers reached over and lowered the flag that had been standing over her dashboard, charging me for every minute in her cab.

"I'm turnin' off the meter," she said.

She drove me into the city, into desolation, and I spread my elbows on the back of her seat as she pointed out the clothing store, Black-owned, the first one broken into, looted, and burned by the rioters. She pointed at a store where a man had gone onto his roof with a hose to try to keep fire from spreading to his business and home, and policemen, assuming him to be a sniper – or so they said – killed him. Then the pawnshop, and the speakeasy – or Blind Pig, as it was called – where it all started with a police raid on the place. One after another. One shell of a building after another. One story after another. And then we came to a two-story brick building that looked like it had survived the brunt of the battle, save some bullet holes in the powdery old bricks.

Sharon pulled the cab street-side. "Do you remember the story in the magazine about the four-year-old girl who was killed?"

"Yes." I could only whisper.

"See that window on the left?" she asked, pointing toward the second story. "Police and soldiers was out here on the street. They said they seen a flash in the window so they started shootin'. What it was, was her daddy was lightin' a cigarette in the darkness of that room. He wa'n't no sniper. They had no cause to start shootin'. That sweet little girl was in her mama's lap, sittin' in a chair on the other side o' that brick wall up there. The bullet went right through them old bricks and right through her baby-chest. Killed her dead."

What else I know now is that it was a .50-caliber bullet that was fired from a tank across the street from that apartment at 1756 West Euclid. I know that thirty minutes after that Wednesday began, July 26, 1967, a tiny girl's life ended, for no good reason. I know that no one was ever held criminally responsible for her death – nor for most of the other forty-three dead and one thousand one hundred and eighty-nine injured during those five days of hell in Detroit, Michigan.

And I know she had a name: Tanya Lynn Blanding.

Tailpiece: For years, a popular rally-cry has been "The South Will Rise Again!" mostly coming from Southerners who won't let the Civil War die. However, recently, it has risen, far beyond the limits of the Confederate flag. Today my home state voted their choice for a Democratic candidate for President of the United States – an African-American man. Previous primaries in South Carolina, Georgia, Alabama, Mississippi, Louisiana, and Virginia also went for Barack Obama, some by close to twice the votes afforded Hillary Clinton. But what touched me most on this day, Tuesday, May 6, 2008, what brought me tears of gratitude and hope in the middle of this writing, was hearing my sister tell me that my fourteen-year-old niece, Hannah, was working at the local Obama headquarters today. How different our childhoods. ... Thank heavens. I am fortunate to be her aunt.

~May 6, 2008~

Chapter 35

Thou Shalt Not Cuss

As far as I was concerned, the entire doctrine of the Foursquare Church could be summed up in one word in the 1940s and '50s: NO.

They started with all the Thou-shalt-nots enumerated in the Ten Commandments, but the church leaders had taken liberties interpreting that list. They told me, along with the other young souls whose lives and life views they were attempting to mold, that it was a sin for girls to wear shorts, for any of us to go to movies or plays, to dance, play cards, curse or take the Lord's name in vain, and to engage in sex before marriage. It took a while to learn that last one was a sin, or to learn about sex at all; it must have been a sin even to talk about it. I learned that whatever we wanted to try, if it was likely to be fun, it was probably wrong. When my classmates went to other dances and to movies after our junior prom, my date and I went to play miniature golf at the local putt-putt. If the powers-that-be had been behind my hooped crinoline skirt when I plucked my golf ball out of the cups, miniature golf would have been added to the list. To this day, I feel awkward trying to dance.

Now, I admit that over the years I learned to cuss like a sailor, but never, ever, ever would I say "fuck" in front of my parents.

Growing up, I had never been allowed even to say "darn." When I tried it once, with my daddy down by the shed, he called me on it and told me not to say it again, it was cussin'.

I said, "Why can't I say 'darn'? *You* cuss."

His denial was prompt as he clipped a glance, and he wouldn't be convinced that the words he used when the hammer hit his thumb or he dropped a wrench or the cow kicked the bucket over came anywhere near cursing. Some arguments can't be won, and I knew I was on the dead end of that one. Yet I never forgot it, and I was never satisfied with the unfairness of it all. I suppose I have spent the rest of my life speaking in a way that has made up for that initial squelching of verbalized emotion.

The two-thousand-mile trip cross country from Tucson to Concord, North Carolina takes four days and a lot of music or audio books to help pass the time. I was making that trek some fifty years later, and for some reason the "darn" day down by the shed with Daddy popped into my mind. I turned off the CD player, opting instead for the mental gyrations of a puzzle that had been waiting to be solved. The miles between Tucson and, oh, El Paso, I'd guess, faded easily with memories of circum-stances that provoked Daddy to say, "Dagnab it!" or

"Gahhh-rait!" – his bywords of frustration. If the annoyance caused extreme exasperation, or pain, "dagnab it" or "gah-rait" weren't strong enough. What he said in the most vexing of situations was "Gahrait t' th' deal fahr!

Gahrait t' th' deal fahr. Once again, all these years later, I was wondering, *what the hell does that mean?*

I had carried the curiosity for so long that I was determined to figure it out by the end of this journey. Using every stretch of inflection I could muster, I repeated the phrase as many times in those four days as Daddy likely had used it during his entire life. No matter how many times I thought it or said it aloud, it still sounded the same – like gibberish – and its meaning eluded me.

By the time I left Birmingham on the morning of the fourth and final five-hundred-mile day, I had slipped into more general memories of Daddy's life. I remembered the pride he felt in belonging to the fire department with its station adjacent to our farm, and I could see the helmet and gear, hanging like a heavy, limp daffodil, inside the water heater closet near the back door, always at the ready for a quick grab when the alarm pierced the country stillness. The men did good work, and even if no emergencies came up, they were always ready to do good work. They also cooked a mean fish fry every now and then and put the money they raised into a fund to help their own if hardship struck. I remembered the years he had worked in the hosiery mill, at one time starting his own in Sanford with a friend, only for it to fail because of full-fashioned stockings giving

211

way to the new fashion of seamless hosiery. I remembered the grueling hours he spent working on the farm, not only on Saturdays, but every day before he went in to work at the mill for his second or third shift stint. I remembered how he could repair anything mechanical and how he let me "help him" by handing him whatever tool he asked for. And I remembered one thing I consider a great gift from him: teaching me carpentry, beginning by letting me, as a kid, help roof a tenant house we were building on our farm. In general, I rolled through those miles remembering how he was "Daddy."

Fifteen hundred miles of these circuitous memories had brought me, by that last day of the trip, to a mahogany plaque that had hung in our house. It honored "Luther Aldridge, Volunteer Fireman of the Year," an accolade dear to him, and, while he was never one to brag, he didn't mind telling people he had been named "Fahrman of the Year." Remembering that plaque and Daddy's pride, as well as his pronunciation, somewhere between Birmingham and Atlanta was where and when the first clue hit me: "fahr." The last part of "Gahrait t' th' deal fahr" must be "fire!"

I laughed out loud. It made perfect sense. I thought, okay, if it ends with fire, what does it start with? Gah. Gah. Gah. God? Yeah, maybe it's God. But there was a big middle of the riddle still to be solved. I had insisted to Daddy that he was cursing, and this, now in my mind, did start with the Lord's name, and surely in vain, I figured. Rait, rait, rait. ...What did that sound like?

"Great" popped out of my mouth, and I now had paired "God" and "great."

So?

I had heard some people say things like "good God!" or "good God a-mighty!" but I wasn't familiar with "great God" as a byword, and this wasn't even "great God." If anything of the kind, it was "God great," and I couldn't figure how that made a lick of sense!

Once the mind is activated, it loves to play – not always to one's advantage – but this time, mine went traveling. It went back to Daddy's ancestral roots and began playing with history and phrasing. Historically, the Scottish and Irish both had made good use of the supernatural in tales told, if not in real life. Stories had been fed from generation to generation by oral traditions that kept cultural remnants, at least, alive, perhaps even in someone so far removed as Daddy. Yet, just as with the game "telephone," where the original whispered sentence may bear little to no semblance to itself by the time it's passed through a dozen children, these stories may have changed, along with their language, as time passed and phrases became more foreign to new users.

Daddy's "t' th'" clearly sounded like "to the." But what was "deal"? What did a deal have to do with fire? Maybe "deal" wasn't deal, but what else could it be? Deal. Deal. De'l. DEVIL! Maybe it was "devil"! Devil fire!

God great to the devil's fire? I rode on for miles with a frown on my face; I was almost weary of my com-

213

mitment to figure this thing out as I turned from Interstate 20 to head north on 85. Then it dawned on me: back then, most curses had counter-curses. Sort of tit-for-tat cursing, I guess. You hand me a curse – that I shall have no peace until I finish some dangerous quest of your bidding – and I toss back the strong suggestion that, until I return, or die, you will stand with one foot on each of two mountain tops and have nothing to eat save what is brought to your mouth by ravens. "Fuck you" would have been so much simpler, if less creative.

"To" and "the" didn't seem so obvious anymore, so I went on with what I thought I knew. I began to say "Gahrait t' th' deal fahr" aloud again, over and over, imagining it this time as a counter-curse, and assuming I was right about god-great-devil-fire as I tried to fill in the blanks. If a curse was the threat of "the devil's fire," what counter-curse might diffuse its power? Well, anybody who believed there was such a thing as fire that a devil was in charge of would also believe in a god – no doubt, a god more powerful than that devil. So, more than likely, they would snap back, "GOD IS GREATER THAN THE DEVIL'S FIRE!"

I pulled into my sister's driveway. *Gahraitt t' th' deal fahr* – I'd finally made it.

~August 15, 2007~

Chapter 36

Voices

My girlfriend was ill. We had been at the 1988
Michigan Womyn's Music Festival where feminists
from all over the United States and many foreign
countries gathered in August every year way up
there in western Michigan. That week, unusual
as it was, hundreds of women, out of perhaps nine
thousand in attendance, fell ill due to water con-
tamination and the resulting outbreak of Shigella.
Nancy was one of those women, one who ended up
in the hospital once we arrived home in Bowling
Green. We had managed to get ourselves and all
our camping gear off the festival land near night-
fall, and I had been doing all the driving while my
sick friend downed yet one more jug of GatorAde.
We both hoped all the way through the middle of
nowhere that she wasn't going to need a restroom or
have to throw up again.

It was close to midnight, and Nancy and I were
driving southeast across Michigan, engrossed in the
most gorgeous lightning show either of us had ever
seen. Directly in front of us were gigantic cumulus
clouds, semi-circling the sky like Japanese paper

lanterns as the bolts danced horizontally from one cloud to the next, lighting up first one and then the next. It was all so beautiful that we were struck dumb: all we could say was "Wow!" over and over. In fact, we were struck dumb enough to forget that we were driving straight into the show, as fast as legally allowed and maybe a bit more, 'cause as I said, Nancy was very sick. As we approached Ann Arbor, which was still an hour and a half from home, tiredness began to overtake me. We had attended the festival for many years, so we knew the road, which meant I knew there was a rest stop just north of Ann Arbor on Highway 23. I told Nancy I had to sleep a few minutes – I've always been very good about being able to pull over when sleepy, sleep for five, ten, fifteen minutes and then be good for more hours. Or minutes, depending on the depth of my aching tiredness. Then I do it all over again, as many times as necessary, to get to where I am going. As important as it was to get home quickly, it was more important to get home, and I told Nancy I had to take a nap.

I pulled into the rest stop, around to the back, and pulled into a parking spot facing a wooded area. I flipped my seat back, pulled my hat down over my eyes, and was asleep before I could remember how sleepy I was. I don't know how long I slept, but it couldn't have been long.

Otherwise totally dead to the world, what woke me – and if you want to think me crazy, go ahead – was a booming voice in my head. It yelled at me (because I'm a sound sleeper or because I'm hardheaded, I don't know), and what it said was, "LEAVE NOW! YOU'RE NOT SAFE HERE!" I sat up immediately, reset my hat firmly, pulled my seat up, started the car, and said to Nancy, "We've got to go!"

She said, "Already? Well, let me go to the restroom first. ..."

"No – you can't! There's no time!" and I explained what I had "heard."

Just as I began to turn my little Corolla wagon onto Highway 23, the proverbial bottom fell out: I'd never seen such rain! Fortunately, I had pulled out directly behind a car whose tail lights I could barely see, because I could not see any sign of the road that I was hoping would stay beneath me – no pavement, no center line, no edge line. My headlights exposed an unmitigated horizontal rain, blasted across us by ferocious winds – and the wind and rain seemed to be a growing force with every inch we crawled. Then – suddenly – just as I was wondering what in the world I should do, the wind shifted, a complete one-eighty, mind you, and the miracle of that split second created a moment of clearness, a stillness that revealed a giant green sign perfectly placed for our reading: ANN ARBOR EXIT. What I'm saying is, if we had been even a smidgen earlier or later than where we were at that very tiny moment in time, the shift in the wind and rain would have offered us nothing – we had seen no other signs due to the curtain of rain, we wouldn't have seen that sign, we wouldn't have seen the ramp. I said, "We're taking it!"

At the bottom of the ramp, there was no street to follow – just a river of rain; water was already up over the curbs and sidewalks. Being a Sunday midnight during a Biblical flood, no fool in her or his right mind would have been out; it was just us in my little car. As we sensed conditions worsening, even though the rain had abated a wee bit, I followed the rain-way toward downtown. I ignored stoplights. The color of them, that is. What couldn't be ignored was the fact that they were being sucked straight up into the air, and I said to Nancy that that didn't seem like a very good sign.

We were coming closer into downtown and large buildings when I spotted a U-shaped arrangement maybe six stories high with a central parking lot. There was hardly a drizzle by then, and we couldn't feel the wind in between the buildings, but I shot to the back of the lot, turned around to be headed out, parked smack-dab in the middle of the lot, and took sight of the potential trajectory of falling bricks if the buildings collapsed in our direction. There was an old orange Mustang parked over against one wall to our right, the only thing in the lot other than our scared-to-death little selves, and in that fearful mind and moment, I could see the wind picking it up and smashing it down right on top of us, even if we escaped burial by bricks. I never turned off the ignition. I don't know why I was so certain we were about to die – as was Nancy – since The Voice obviously had saved us back at the rest area. It hadn't said, "LEAVE NOW! YOU'RE NOT SAFE HERE! BUT I'M GOING TO TAKE YOU TO WHERE YOU REALLY WILL DIE!"

I had been way too busy even to be thinking about that, and besides, it seemed like a lifetime ago. So, since we were about to die, we held hands and said how much we loved each other, how fortunate our friendship was, if we had to die now we were glad we could do it together. All that stuff. And not one brick or Mustang fell.

The next day, I went to work after taking Nancy to her doctor, who hospitalized her.

Art Department faculty members dropped by my office regularly to chat, and that morning Ralph Warren came in. Ralph had friends in Ann Arbor and I suppose he had talked to someone that morning, because he casually sipped his coffee and said to me, "Did you hear about that bad storm that hit Ann Arbor last night?"

"Hear about it? Nancy and I were IN it!"

He said, "You were? Did you know two campers got killed when a tornado hit behind the rest area north of town?"

~August 10, 2009~

Chapter 37

Blue

The world I lived in expected a girl graduating from high school to marry, settle down, and get busy cleaning house, changing diapers, and catering to her husband's every whim, but a few of us in my tiny graduating class of forty-four students decided instead to go to college. Not only did I not want any part of that "homemaking" plan, I wouldn't have known how to live that way. I had spent my eighteen years as a full-tilt tomboy, had no interest in girl-y things, and hardly knew how to be one.

So 1960, the first of my college years, became one of major compromise for me. What I loved was art, but having had no opportunity to study it in high school, I felt I lacked sufficient "background." Therefore, I decided to major in home economics. The field gloried in the claim that it was "the career with a thousand-and-one job titles," so I figured I would find something I would love to do. I also figured I would learn how to "be a girl." With the degree did come skills that most young women cherished as homemakers – but it didn't change me into one of those women. Between that graduation and eventually returning to school years later to study art, I explored several of those thousand-and-one job titles and enjoyed them all: they allowed me to teach, travel, and be creative.

The first adventure was as a teacher in Elizabeth City's Central High School in northeastern North Carolina. I had come to love that part of the state while student teaching in the neighboring village of Hertford. I had had a helpful supervising teacher, Frances Newby who, along with her elderly parents (who more or less adopted me), lived in a spotless old Victorian house on the banks of the Perquimans River, and I spent many a day and night in that home and on their pier that crawled far out into the river. The river narrows to a small channel on the north side of town, and at that point it is spanned by an S-curved bridge that was built in the 1920s and is claimed to be the oldest of its kind in the world. It was soon after that, so folks say, that Benny Davis noticed a gigantic harvest moon as he was crossing the bridge. The sight of the moon over the dark river stopped him in his tracks and, homesick for his sweetheart, he penned the lyrics to "Carolina Moon."

I have a lot of fond memories of those months in Hertford – including the pride of Hertford, Jimmy "Catfish" Hunter (Oakland A's and Yankees pitcher), being in my study hall and his future wife, Helen, in my home economics class.

Much like the Hertford students had been, my very own students at Central came primarily from farm families, sometimes missing school because they

222

were needed at home when the hay needed cutting or the hogs needed killing or the vegetables needed canning. Most of the girls married as soon as they graduated – if they hadn't already quit school for that purpose. The land edging the Great Dismal Swamp provided a wealth of farmland and forests of cypress and pine and oak. Many of the boys left school, diploma in hand or not, to follow in their fathers' furrows or to work in the logging industry. I remember a damp, gray Monday morning when one of my best students had a visitor come to the door with a message. Her fiancé, who had graduated the spring before, and had been driving a log truck to save money for their new home had set out that day in a dense fog that was normal on those fall mornings; he had stopped for a car that had stopped in front of him, but the truck behind him couldn't tell Bo's truck wasn't moving, plowed into the back of him, and Bo's load of logs went right through the cab of his truck, removing Bo's head on the way. She didn't finish out the year. I don't recall her name, but I doubt I will ever forget her face or that day.

The classroom was just that: a regular classroom, no larger than one with a simple collection of desks, yet ours was crammed with four kitchen units, four study tables that seated the eighteen or twenty students that crowded into each class, and, lining the meager wall space, stacks of sewing machines that filled the floor space part of the year when we stacked the tables instead of the machines. During the "sewing units," we laid broomsticks across the kitchens' wall cabinets for makeshift "closets" so the girls in the half dozen classes would have a place to

223

hang their sewing projects.

The girls who took home ec were required to turn in a "home project" – something that might be compared today to a Girl Scout earning a badge. The project could be based in any of the many topics we covered in class, and it needed to be something that would benefit their family or community. We studied foods (including the chemistry of cooking), sewing, home management (finances, etc.), child care, health, and housing, among other topics. The girls turned in monthly progress reports, and the grading was a royal pain to keep up with. I rented a room from a widow in town and one side of my bed invariably was stacked with six tall piles of file folders thick with intentions and proofs, a stack for each class. I slept like death itself and never did one folder fall off a stack. Mrs. Stanley finally admitted to me that she was no longer changing my sheets once a week – she just turned them around for the second week.

I had to visit each student, at home, to discuss her project with her and her parent(s), so each nine months I went into nearly a hundred homes scattered around the flat farms and beautiful waterways of Pasquotank County. One of those homes was blue, and I can attest to the fact that there was not another electric blue house in all of Pasquotank County. I suspect one would have had to travel as far as Taos Pueblo's doors to see that particular hue anywhere else. It stood out.

So did my student who lived there.

I never knew very much about Eula Faye's home

life. She didn't talk about any siblings or her parents, and there was no other family member at home whenever I visited her. I somehow felt their absence was on purpose. Shyness? Embarrassment? I don't know. Eula Faye embodied her share of strangeness and perhaps the rest of her kin did, too.

In stature, she was a sturdy sort. Not fat, mind you, just sort of square. Not tall, either, maybe five-five, but broad shoulders, a square face with a bold jaw line, and the thick socks and brogans that she wore with her usually-plaid cotton full skirts and limp but thick crinolines, year 'round, made her look – well – sturdy. She was always clean, and her hair was nearly always neat, although her 'do was a style many years older than she was: she, or one of those relatives I never saw, must have rolled tight little curls in the front and sides and back of her head, nightly, and some mornings she arrived at school with curlers gone but without a brush or comb having touched her head.

But the oddest thing about Eula Faye was her eyes. Except for being paler, they were well nigh the same blue as her house. They appeared hollow. And they were haunting.

My brother-in-law says that in the South we think we can report any unflattering characteristic of a person so long as we preface the statement with "bless her heart." Well – bless her heart – Eula Faye was not very bright. Her records showed an IQ of about 70, indicative of mild mental retardation. While I don't mean that as a condemnation, I'm simply reporting it as fact, and it was also fact back then that mental retardation was seen by many people as a really bad thing, way beyond "unflattering." In spite of that – or perhaps because of it – Eula Faye carried herself with perfect posture and walked as a young woman of high confidence and hope.

No, Eula Faye wasn't very smart, but she was mighty sweet, and for some unknown reason she loved me to no end. She never missed a class, and at lunchtime and while awaiting her turn for a bus ride home, she'd always come to my classroom and ask if I needed any help. Could she sweep? Could she carry out the trash? Could she straighten up my desk? She always wanted to help. My first year at Central, she did not pass home ec. No matter how big the A for effort, I just could not justify passing her. Undaunted, she signed up for it again the next year.

So, it was Eula Faye's second time around, and we were immersed in the health unit. I had tackled my lesson plans with a certain degree of trepidation: body-talk was not an easy subject in 1964, many topics and words being taboo in "polite company," definitely so in mixed company; I knew I could possibly expect visits from strict parents who did not approve of some things being discussed in the classroom. These girls were well into their menstrual years, and the menses were acknowledged every way but forthrightly – my period, that time of the month, Aunt Flo(w) is here, I can't go swimming, seeing red, the cramps, the curse, on the rag, the pip, my red-headed aunt is visiting, granny's visiting, I'm sick, or, as my Grandma Aldridge used to ask me, "Is your monkey's nose bleeding?" – I might as well have said, "Go away! I'm having my euphemism!"

Still, there was a likelihood that few of the girls had been given The Talk about where babies come from. Or how. I certainly intended my approach toward body awareness, sex, and health to be years and miles away from Pat Boone's Puritan stance in his 1958 book "Twixt Twelve and Twenty" (published while I was in high school) – sort of a how-to guide to being a "good" adolescent. From Pat Boone, of all people. Puhleeze!! I was aware that I would have to walk and talk a fine line: I would just present the facts, ma'am, and keep it as scientific as possible.

For the purpose of advertising – rather than prose-lytizing, like Mr. White Buck Shoes had done – the Kotex folks put out some reasonably good teaching aids back then: charts, filmstrips, booklets. After all, it was still the era of those god-awful elastic belly-belts with dangling shrapnel, through which we threaded and anchored the tail-ends of the pads those few days once a month. As if cramps weren't torture enough. The Kotex, Kimberly-Clark, Modess, and Mydol companies were more interested, of course, in promoting their pins, pads, and pills than just educating, but their materials were helpful and appreciated. The Modess advertising tag was "Modess...because" – because "feminine hygiene" was loaded with unmentionables. The health unit was underway. Of course word had traveled, and boys were seen to dawdle and dally outside our door during those weeks, peeking in, grinning, and pretending they weren't the roosters in a henhouse. Soon, the entire student body was in heat. I had charts on the wall – NOT to be seen from the door-way – that illustrated female and male bodies, and

I had been teaching them about the reproductive organs. I assumed the boys' similar education happened only in the locker room.

One day I clearly pointed out on the chart the female's three openings ("down there") and carefully explained their functions. The next day, Eula Faye raised her hand and I called on her. She hemmed and hawed, squirmed in her seat, played with her crinoline, and finally said, "I have a question but I'm afraid to ask it." I assured her she could safely ask anything she wanted. "But I'm afraid people will laugh at me."

Knowing there was a risk of that – particularly since these young girls could become giggly and twitter on and on around this topic and because Eula Faye was Eula Faye – I gave the class a sideways order: "Eula Faye, we won't laugh at you. We might laugh *with* you, but we won't laugh at you. Go ahead and ask whatever you want."

Eula Faye said, "Didn't you tell us we have three openings down there?"

"Yes – "

"Well, I can't find but two!" And the class erupted.

I said, "Now, just hush, just hush! At least I know which one of you did her homework last night!"

Bless her heart.

~February 28, 2009~

Chapter 38

Ladies(?) and Gentleman

I was a senior at East Carolina at the time, in Greenville, North Carolina. I received a phone call from my Aunt "Twogun" saying she had met a nice young man on a bus who was from a tiny town near Greenville and recently out of the Army. She told him about me, he said he'd like to meet me, and she had given him my number. Oh, for god's sake! I had not yet learned that there was a name for who I was – "lesbian" – I just knew that I did not enjoy, nor want, the company of males the way "other girls" did, so this held absolutely no interest for me. Maybe my aunt did know who I was and was trying to "fix" me; I don't know. For sure, she meant well and was trying to "fix me up." You may safely consider as fact that I grew up as a "good" child. I was taught to live by the Golden Rule. And did. It came as a great surprise to me that I could express even the slightest bit of guile.

He called. He asked if I'd like to go out, quickly adding that I should feel free to bring a friend along, because after all, he said, I didn't know him. Well, I guess if he could kill one young woman, he could as easily kill two, but back then those things weren't thought of as much as now. Not by me, anyway. I told him I would think about going out with him, for him to call me back the next week. He had given me an easy opening to a mendacious side I didn't know I had. I ran back to my room where my two roommates were waiting for the scoop, and I told them my plan, but it would have to involve one of them. I told them that I would take him up on the offer to take a friend along – but I wanted us to switch identities. Joan jumped at the chance.

I've got to tell you, the two of us could not have been more different. Back then I was a long drink of water: I was five-nine and a half, a hundred and twenty-eight pounds with clothes on, and I could see all three hip and pubic bones when flat on my back. Joan was maybe five-four and never saw a hundred pounds. I was tailored; she was frilly. I was a tomboy; she was prissy. And we sounded nothing alike. Still, the two of us set the plan in motion. We studied each other's backgrounds, she having to learn more about mine than I about hers, because we had no idea what my aunt had told him – family, church, hobbies, all that. We practiced trying to pitch our voices closely, mine up, hers down, paid attention to the tempo and the accents. When the next phone call came, we were both in the phone booth. (Yes, a phone booth in the dorm lobby; this was a long time ago, folks.) We held the receiver between our ears so we could both hear what he said; we took turns answering him. We needed more time: I put him off for another week. And another.

More practice, more study. More trading of responses during each week's conversation. We should've hit the books as diligently.

When date time finally arrived – well, suffice it to say that while Henry may have unleashed my dormant, conniving side, he had not obliterated my innate wussiness: I wanted to chicken out, but Joan was so into this by now there was no way she would not have her chance on stage. We compromised: I, "Joan," would go along as "Carol's" friend, but, so sorry, "Joan" had come down with laryngitis. Only when she confused and misstated some information that I considered critical to my real identity would I, through fake raspy whispers, say something to change the subject. More often, I just jabbed my elbow into her ribs.

It was the longest night of my life.

After a couple hours in his car, all of us jammed together on the bench seat, and then dinner, he excused himself to the restroom. I told Joan that her "Carol" had to end this fiasco. It had begun to dawn on me that I really had no idea what or how much my aunt had told him about me – and I recalled, suddenly, that she had told me he had a sister at EC; I knew he was bound to have looked me up in her yearbooks. Who wouldn't? Why had I not remembered that? With that realization, I was mortified. I thought I had masterminded The Great Farce. Now I was just sorry that I had been so deceitful to a simple country boy who obviously had much better manners than I. I realized I had simply been stupid, and unbelievably inconsiderate

231

and unkind, and this young man, more than likely, had known all along what I was doing and exercised his Southern Gentleman Gene so as not to embarrass me and my friend. He had to know what we had done, and he never let on, not even when the evening ended.

 Perhaps he did recognize me from a photograph; perhaps my aunt had shown him one on the bus. The thing he could not have known was that he had gone to a mighty amount of effort for a date with someone who never had the courage to own up to her own moronic hoax, let alone apologize.

He kept calling for several weeks and I never even went to the phone.

~April 26, 2010~

Chapter 39

OW!

I grab the steering wheel and although it has a covering, it is so hot it burns my hands. I keep trying to hold on in spite of the discomfort – no, not discomfort; it's pain. Real pain. "Ow! Ow!"

Some things are like that. Just too hot. Some situations, some circumstances are like that. Too hot for comfort. Some people are like that, too. So hot, in one way or another, that it's hard to hold onto them. Or to know if you want to.

So I drive on, navigating by my fingernails, reminded that a cooling off is sometimes the only salvation and that vigilance is an essential self-indulgence.

~May 9, 2010~

Chapter 40

Dipso-Patsy

It was 1967. Just before Thanksgiving. Just before my birthday. I arrived in Buffalo. It was my last assignment working for The McCall Pattern Company; I hadn't wanted to go there, didn't want to be there, was feeling generally pissed, and, I guess, maybe, just a wee bit mean. It was cold, it was snowing, it was dreary, I had officially quit my job, but reluctantly had agreed to do this one last two-week stint.

My mountain of personal and McCall's bags had been wheeled from baggage and stuffed into the rear of the limo-taxi, and I crawled into the seat behind the driver; an obnoxious drunk got into the seat behind me. Slurring instructions to the driver, he suddenly noticed the neck of the case beside me – my baritone uke that I traveled with to keep me sane on the road.

"Oh! Do you play violin?"

The case looked nothing like a violin case. "Yes," I decided to say, lying more quickly than I care to admit.

"Wow – are you in Buffalo for a concert?"

"Yes."

He was getting more excited and draping part of himself over my seat, an intrusion, by my measure, that justified my deception.

"Where?"

"Kleinhans Music Hall," I thankfully remembered. I knew of the place only because I'd flown in beside a pianist who *was* going to perform there.

"When?" My unwelcome companion was nearly breathless with excitement.

"Tuesday night at eight."

"GOD! I LOVE VIOLIN!!" His obnoxious breath was as loud as his voice.

I turned to look him in the eye.

"You do? Then why don't you show up at the ticket window Tuesday night – there'll be a ticket waiting for you."

How proud Daddy would be, I thought, the champion of the no-real-lie: there *would* be tickets at the ticket window – tickets for something. The drunk was elated. And probably too drunk to remember to go, let alone to remember that I never even asked for his name.

~August 29, 2008~

Chapter 41

Call to Duty

When I moved here in 1991, it appeared that Tucson's four-hundred-thousand-plus population consisted of four hundred thousand people who were retired, and the "plus" consisted of the few among us who were still working. That's what began to tick me off by the third time within a year that I was called to jury duty, even though my group number was spared the first two times and I wasn't required to show up at all. I know – civic duty, it's an honor and responsibility to serve, and all that stuff – but why was I being called so many times when there were thousands "free" to serve?

There is a delicious piece of desert in Tucson that used to be home to Dick and Jean Wilson, a couple who early on foresaw the city's future and placed the property in a trust that eventually created Tohono Chul Park. As the Wilsons foresaw and predicted, it has come to be surrounded by the northern sprawl of the city. Locals and visitors flock to this oasis to learn about the flora of the Sonoran Desert along the well-planned and informative paths etched throughout the park, to buy plants from the greenhouse or souvenirs in the shops, to attend classes on various subjects, to attend exhibitions in the art gallery, and to attend concerts in the small amphitheatre. The Wilsons' home was transformed into one of the gift shops and a restaurant that serves gourmet meals and an afternoon tea with scones and almond tea good enough to write home about.

The Wilsons owned an independent bookstore, and during its incarnation it moved three times, the last move establishing it into a new building on the edge of Tohono Chul Park. Called The Haunted Bookshop, it was a general bookstore, not one filled only with mysteries as the name might hint. The shop's name came from Christopher Morley's book of the same title in which he said, and I'm paraphrasing, "I am haunted by all the books I have not read."

Popular not only locally, The Haunted was famous, preferred by many delighted and loyal customers in the United States and abroad. Customer service was excellent. One of its most unique and popular features was the "tunnel": a small "underground" room at the bottom of a ramp. It was stocked with children's books and stuffed animals. When parents came to the shop with kids in tow, the wee ones ran straight for the tunnel where they remained while equally pleased parents wandered around the shop to their hearts' content, not having to worry a moment about their children. A glass top over the tunnel allowed curious parents to observe their happily occupied children, playing with items provided by The Haunted and with other children provided by other parents.

Then "big box bookstores" came to town, the first one only a mile or so from The Haunted. They knew their competition. Or their target, as the Wilsons felt the truth to be. The Haunted closed not long after that invasion, as did many independents around the country.

During my second year in Tucson, I started working there, and I'd be hard pressed to say I ever enjoyed any work more than my time at The Haunted Bookshop. My co-workers were fun, funny, intelligent, and dedicated to the customers and the shop. We each had our shelf sections, or genres, that we were in charge of keeping an eye on and maintaining their order. I soon learned which customers bought what from my sections, and I would call a regular and say, "A new [so-and-so] just came in. I'll hold a copy for you – you do not want to miss this one!" I started at minimum wage and never got paid a lot more than that, which in itself meant I went home with very little money. What made my take-home really meager was the tempting and often-used 40 percent discount on books.

In 1992 when I saw a new title pop out at me from a face-out near the cash register, I ran for it. One of my favorite writers, Southern and otherwise, claimed to be a gun-totin' Republican lesbian. Those first two labels strike me as belonging together; the last two never make sense to me at all. But since Florence King is one of my written-word heroes, I take her at her word. Along with most of May Sarton's, my personal library holds copies of nearly all her books now, offering me the occasional and happy rereading. One of the funniest books I ever read is her **Confessions of a Failed Southern Lady**. When her new book caught my eye that day, it meant I'd go home with at least an hour's less pay.

So when that third jury summons was in my hand, I called a telephone number, as all potential jurors are instructed to do, to hear a recording that would tell me whether my group had to show up the next day. As they say, third time's a charm: my group had to report. I went to the Pima County Courthouse on the appointed day instead of to the Haunted Bookshop. There must have been five hundred of us, like cattle in a holding pen, with everyone waiting, patiently or not, reading their John Grisham novels. Except for me. I was reading my precious new Florence King.

Once inside the courtroom, late in the afternoon, the judge began asking if anyone was there who felt they shouldn't serve on this jury. Mine was not the only hand that went up. In turn, she called me to the bench and I proceeded to explain:

"First, I have to say that I am missing work to be here. If I miss work, I do not get paid. If I have to be here even another day, I will not be able to pay all my bills this month. Second, I overheard the lawyers talking, so I know this joker was caught speeding – drunk – already on a suspended license for the same offense, that there was a wreck and someone was hurt or killed – I didn't hear clearly which. Third, I have absolutely no patience with drunk driving! So I can tell you, in all honesty, that if I have to stay here and miss any more work and miss paying my bills because of some little twit of an asshole who was caught driving drunk – again! – and hurt or killed somebody in the process, I am going to be ROYALLY PISSED!"

The robed woman's mouth was twitching, squelching a smile, as she thanked me for my candor and excused me from her courtroom. If my argument was convincing, it must have been upped a notch by Florence King's book that I held in my folded arms, title toward the judge: **With Charity Toward None: A Fond Look at Misanthropy.**

~April 18, 2008~

Chapter 42

Calling the Colors

As wondrous as the science of it is, dental procedures can be brutal. Brutally painful, not to mention brutally expensive. Recently, I sat for three and a quarter hours and I endured two root canals and six crowns. Gratefully, I hasten to add, in spite of the pain. I also counted a total of thirteen shots, but I'm not sure that I might've missed some in the count.

Going to the dentist is – no surprise – not one of my favorite ways to spend a morning. But I decided on some ways to make it as tolerable as possible. I took my iPad with me and in between the times of being worked on, I started reading Fannie Flagg's book that I downloaded the night before – and that gave me some actual laughs. Normally laughs are pretty hard to come by in a dentist's chair. The other thing I did? Well, I wondered if I could allow it to be a bit of a "Zen experience."

I was really getting into that until Dr. Johnson surprised me with five more shots, and I heard coming from me what I knew was meant to be the words "Oh Jesus!" through gauze rolls, water sprays, and suction tubes. I have hard fingernails. ROCK hard. So when I have to deal with dental work, I tend to press my thumbnail into another fingertip – until it hurts. That gives me a bit of a choice of which pain to focus on. I'll take the fingertip pain any time. And during these last shots, I fully suspected all my fingertips would need stitches by the time we were done. But back to the Zen experience. ...

You see, I see colors. With my eyes shut, that is. Not always, but sometimes. My history of this goes back to when I was about thirteen and at a church summer camp in the hills of northern Georgia and was filled with the Holy Spirit. I was kneeling, praying, eyes closed, and I started "seeing" a beautiful blue – something close to a Carolina blue sky. I opened my eyes, only to see the rafters of the underside of the roof of the outdoor shelter where this service was being held. Closing my eyes again, colors began to churn. I've always described them as though someone dropped food coloring into a vat of water, a vat like a bingo or lottery tub, dropping a tiny bit of one color at a time, so that one sort of bled into the one before, all pastels. Needless to say, I was aware of this being quite a special phenomenon. The Colors didn't return until much later in my life when – are you ready for this? – I was having orgasms on a fairly regular basis. The Colors seemed so normal to me that I figured everybody saw them when making love. Until I began to ask. To this day, I've met only a few people who see them.

The Colors have always seemed to me to be some sort of message, or some kind of communication, so I began to wonder if I could "call them" at will, and

I began to test that curiosity when I'd go to see doctors. By then, The Colors had come to have individual meanings for/to me, the green being a very healing hue. Mind you, these colors are not like any I know of in real life; the green is close to an emerald green, but not exactly. And when I "call them," they are rarely pastel; they are quite bold. I soon learned that when I called them during a doctor's appointment, if the green came, I knew this doctor and I would be working together toward a healing. There was one visit, however, that was quite the contrary. I was waiting for a doctor whom I had not seen before; I was on the table, gown on, waiting for him to come in to examine me, and I thought, "I should call The Colors. ..." When I did, all I saw was a deep brown that looked like shit sliding down a wall. I got off the table, dressed, went out to the front desk, and told the receptionist that I was cancelling the appointment. No way I wanted to meet that guy, let alone have him touch me!

I must say, I had never, ever before this recent appointment thought about calling The Colors during a dental procedure. But, right in the middle of all the drilling and worst pain, I thought to do it. And there they were! All pastels again, like the first time. I'd normally be hard-pressed to call going to a dentist a spiritual experience, but, frankly, I do think that pain is.

~September 23, 2014~

Chapter 43

The Women's Department

Grandma Aldridge loved to go – go anywhere. So if one of her kids she was staying with at the time needed to go shopping, she was probably the first one in the car. Mind you, by that time she could hardly see or hear, but none of that was to slow Grandma down. She would wind her way through the aisles of dresses, touching each one and, going by "feel," she'd say, "Oh, ain't that purty!" When she got tired she'd find a chair to sit in and rest while my aunt finished shopping.

Such chairs were scattered about primarily for the convenience of husbands who had been dragged along on shopping trips. Women's departments back then had floor-length mirrors where women would come out of the dressing rooms to view the dress they had tried on and seek husband approval. So one particular day Grandma found a chair, and later she told me what had happened. She said that she hadn't noticed when the other woman came over to where she was and sat opposite her, but she turned around and realized she was no longer alone. She said to me, "I said 'hello' to her and she spoke back – of course I couldn't hear her, but I saw her lips moving. She was real nice, smiled at me a lot. I tried to carry on a conversation with her but soon stopped, 'cause I was kind of embarrassed that I couldn't hear her. And you know what else? She was wearing a dress about the same pretty pink as mine! I told her I really liked her dress 'cause I do love pink."

Then Grandma leaned in toward me and said in not much more than a whisper, "Do you know I was talkin' to myself in a mirror the whole time?"

~April 29, 2017~

Chapter 44

Travels with Grandma

I am fascinated by the arrival of memories. I don't know how it happens, or why, but whatever it is that springs from deep recesses among the brain synapses – well, I'm thankful for it. Traveling with Grandma Aldridge and Lori popped into my consciousness when I started to go to sleep again this morning at seven thirty and I drifted off, smiling.

The first memory that burst into my mind this morning must've been lurking there since 1968 because I was living in Elizabeth City, North Carolina, working at Virginia Electric & Power Company, and living out on the Angus farm. My little sister was only eight years old at the time, and she and Grandma Aldridge, who would've been seventy-three years old then, were visiting me during the summer. One day I woke up with a bright idea: I asked Grandma to make some of her famous potato salad; I made some sandwiches and deviled eggs. The next morning, we got up early, packed a picnic basket with plates and utensils and chips, put the potato salad and sandwiches and eggs into a cooler with a bunch of Pepsis, I'm sure, and headed north. Grandma Aldridge never ever wasted a breath getting to the car if someone said, "Let's go!" Anywhere!

It was only a four-hour drive to Washington, DC and I wanted to show them the monuments and, in particular, to take them to the Smithsonian. I have only one memory of being inside the Smithsonian, and that was to stand for a long time staring at the Hope Diamond. Lori remembers that we went to the gift shop and that I told her she could pick one item for me to buy for her. She had a hard time deciding between little honor guard figures from Buckingham Palace and a prism. She picked the figures, and fifty-two years later she still regrets not having chosen the prism.

But what I do remember as though it happened yesterday was what we did on the grounds. I had also packed a quilt and a pillow. I laid the quilt in front of a gigantic oak tree and placed a pillow against the trunk so Grandma could sit there and comfortably lean back against it. We unloaded our cooler and basket and chowed down in great style, amongst the ghosts of this country's history.

Also on the grounds was a magnificent carousel that had been installed the year before. Lori and I could hardly wait to finish eating so we could ride, but Grandma had no interest in "going round and round on that thing!" until we finally talked her into getting on and riding in one of the bench seats. We nearly had to drag her off the thing! I lost count of how many times she kept riding.

We put our goodies back in the car, pointed it south, and got home by bedtime, after a full day of happy family time.

Five years passed and I was living in eastern North Carolina; Lori and Grandma were again visiting me. That time the "bright idea" was to take them to Charleston, South Carolina for the weekend because it was only three hours away. The eastern side of both those Carolina states have areas that are timber-heavy, and at one point we found ourselves driving down a highway lined on both sides with such tall trees we could barely see any sky. Grandma thought those were the most beautiful trees she'd ever seen! Miles later, and still squeezed by the woods, she was saying, "My goodness, there sure are a lot of trees here..." And if you knew Grandma, you'd know she never said something just once – she went on and on and on about those trees. More miles and feeling nearly suffocated by them, I guess, she eventually was saying, "Will we ever get out of these woods?"

The meat of the trip was to be a visit out to Fort Sumter, which happens to be the site of the first shots fired in the Civil War. I'm no fan of battle history, Civil War or any others, but forts as architecture I do find interesting. What I had thought, above all, was that Lori and Grandma would enjoy the idea of a boat trip out to the fort. Wrong. Grandma swore and be-damned – well, Grandma would never do either, but she was adamant about not intending to get onto that boat! We said everything we could to try to convince her, and the only thing that finally

251

did the trick was to show her I had already spent money on our three tickets. Still reluctant, she gingerly boarded the gangplank. It was chilly on the water, and she had her coat buttoned up, her scarf around her head, and she didn't have anything to say on the way across the water.

We walked around after arriving on the little island, and Lori and I told Grandma we wanted to go inside and look at the dungeons, did she want to come along? No. So we found her a convenient bench where she could watch the water and the tourists and wait for us. When we came back outside, Grandma had certainly found her voice: she had a gaggle of folks around her as she entertained them with goodness knows what sorts of stories, and she was happy as a lark!

The next morning we got up with plans to look around Charleston, and once we got into town, Grandma handed me a twenty and said, "Now, Baby, you can take this money and get us tickets to go out on that boat again."

Once was enough. "A gracious plenty," in fact, as we tend to say down home.

~March 15, 2017~

252

Chapter 45

Friendly Fur

I've been thinking about all the precious critters that have paraded through my life. I've told about the first love of my life, a collie named Lassie – of course – in a story about living in Sanford, North Carolina; she was my seven-year-old self's best friend and she died a sad and painful death.

Lassie Number Two

A few years later we were living on our farm between Concord and Charlotte and I had another "Lassie" as well as her mother, Queen. Daddy didn't believe in animals living in the house, so, much to my chagrin, both dogs lived outside, chained to dog houses year 'round. One cold, rainy April Saturday, Lassie began giving birth. First to one little puppy, then another, and another…eventually twelve pups in all! Daddy had given me a cardboard box with towels in it and told me to turn the oven to "warm" and set the box on the oven door, open toward that warmth. As each pup was delivered, Daddy ran into the house and put it into the box. The twelfth one was born dead. I had never seen my daddy moving so fast – he ran into the kitchen, laid the puppy on the red linoleum counter, and began giving him artificial respiration. He massaged that little baby's chest until he started breathing! Before the puppies were old enough to sell, we kept the whole clan, Grandma, Mama, and babies, in our utility room. Daddy put together a little corral of sorts, about four by six feet, outlined by two-inch by six-inch boards, and padded it with "cotton sheets." Not the kind you and I sleep between at night – these were large sheets, about twelve feet square, made by sewing feed sacks together. Sheets like these were laid at the end of rows of cotton so workers could empty their sacks full of picked cotton onto them; then the sheets would have the corners pulled to the center, tied in a knot, and lifted by the tractor's hydraulic lift with an attached scale to weigh the day's pickings. Now, on this off-season day of multiple births, the sheets served a special purpose. We kept Daddy's resurrected treasure, Prince, and one of his little sisters, Lady. After a few months spent finding homes for the little ones, our remaining collie family had shrunk from fourteen members to four.

I remember one day I was outside and heard the youngsters, maybe a year old by then, barking at a back corner of the house. I saw what they were barking at and called Daddy to come see the coiled snake hiding under the downspout. Although Daddy respected black and king snakes because they did good things on the farm, he didn't want any near the house. His way of killing a snake was to jerk it up by the tail, swing it round and round, and snap it like a whip; I assume that broke its neck, although it's hard to think of a snake having a neck – or maybe having anything but a neck. He told me to run to the far end of the yard so I'd be out of the way of his murderous plan. But when he snapped the snake, a fang flew from its mouth and to this day I have a tiny scar on my left wrist where it struck me. What are the odds?

I was a freshman in high school when Lassie, the Lassie who had had the twelve babies, disappeared for a couple days. I was heartsick without my best friend, and I was horrified when she did come home: she was full of buckshot. We never had proof, but we thought a man on a neighboring farm had shot her; foxes had been raiding his chickens and it would have been easy enough to mistake Lassie's small size and color for a fox in dim lighting or among the shadows in the woods. Thankfully, she survived. The man on the neighboring farm had no idea how much I despised him, guilty or not.

DC

By 1968 I had quit the job with The McCall Pattern Company and moved back to Elizabeth City, North Carolina where I had once taught home economics in the county high school. This time, though, I was the new home economist for Virginia and Electric and Power Company. There was a specially equipped room just off the main office. It wasn't only a kitchen, it was also a small auditorium of sorts. People would come in, invariably women, for demonstrations that I would give, preparing recipes for different electrical appliances. The demo table had an overhead mirror so the audience could clearly see what I was doing on the tabletop. Back then, there was a new-fangled device showing up in some "better" kitchens: the microwave oven. And our job – well, my job, in this case – was to convince people they needed anything and everything that would cause them to use more electricity. That first microwave in my VEPCO kitchen was a monstrously big one by today's standards. It was an Amana Radarange.

The microwave oven had been created rather by accident in 1945 at the end of World War II by a worker at Raytheon, Percy Spencer, who, believe it or not, had only a grammar school education. The first commercial ones in 1947 were about the size of a refrigerator and cost three thousand dollars, so mostly they were sold to hotels and ships, not to your average homeowner. Then in 1967, Amana, a company that had been bought by Raytheon, made the countertop Radarange available to anyone who could afford the four-hundred-ninety-five-dollar price tag. At first sound that might not seem at all unreasonable for such a newfangled luxury, but remember – four hundred ninety-five dollars in 1967 would be the same as thirty-six hundred dollars in 2016.

Nevertheless, there one sat, in my kitchen at VEPCO. I read the manual religiously, because I had to learn to use the thing, even with some trepidation. And to tell the truth, that old monster was a lot more interesting, in useful ways, than the microwaves today. For instance, as Thanksgiving and Christmas approached, the mirrored demonstrations didn't involve just food, but holiday decorations as well. And for the little crowds that came to learn about new decorations and sweets I had to serve refreshments. SaraLee made a little pound cake, about nine inches long, a rectangular sweet in an aluminum foil pan. Not only could I pop that whole thing, foil container included, into the Radarange, from rock-hard frozen to steaming hot in four minutes flat, I could also do something mighty fancy with a beef roast! I covered one third of the roast in foil; then, covering that part again, I wrapped a total of two thirds of the roast, leaving one third uncovered. I don't remember the number of minutes I put on the dial, but after the first round of minutes, I removed the foil that covered the second third of the roast, and then put the same number of minutes on the dial again. Finally, unwrapping the final third, the first-wrapped, I cooked the roast again. Why all that? Because I ended up with a beef roast that could satisfy three different preferences – well done, medium, and rare. DO NOT try this at home! Not with the microwave ovens of today unless you want to blow them up.

You think I digress? Well, I do and I don't. After all, I am a Southerner telling a story. There's a point to our tangents, and there is a point to this one, too.

Within less than a hundred-mile radius of my VEPCO office were two others. Barbara Rogers was the home economist down in Robersonville; I don't remember the name of the other woman in this tale; I don't even remember where her office was. Rocky Mount, I believe. Whatever her name, the three of us headed off one day in my company sedan for Washington, DC to attend a company-wide meeting. What I do remember about that other woman is that her husband was a pig farmer. At one point, driving up Interstate 95, we found ourselves trapped behind an eighteen wheeler hauling hogs to market. Say what you will, animals on their way to slaughter know what they face – they know whether it is going to be humane or not, and usually it is the inhumane version of death they are headed toward. Having grown up around a lot of this, I can tell you, the more fear, the more shit. Being behind those scared pigs on a sweltering summer day in a car with no air conditioning was brutal! Barbara and I were complaining – and gagging – and the nameless one just kept saying, "Ummm, smells like money to me!"

The meeting we finally attended doesn't matter, what matters is what we did before leaving town to go back to North Carolina. I had been thinking about getting a dog, but Elizabeth City held slim pickings. So – I told my traveling companions I wanted to find a dog shelter before we left town. We drove to the northeast side of the city to a huge shelter. One of the cages inside was bigger than my bedroom; there must've been a hundred dogs in it! I stood looking at them all as they jumped against the wire, barking their begging to be chosen. Suddenly I noticed one dog. This one caught my attention because he sat—sat! mind you—quiet as a mouse in a back corner, apart from all the rowdy ones who were

desperately clamoring up front, and he had a knowing, peaceful look on his face, and he was staring
right into my eyes. I thought, "Oh, man! That is
one smart dog! He knows full well what he's doing!"
I turned to the attendant and said, "I'll take that one
in the corner!" The people at the shelter told me that
DC (what else could I have named him?) was just
a couple years old; they told me he had belonged to
a family whose home had burned and they couldn't
take the dog with them to the place they were moving.
Wow – how heartbreaking for all of them, to be
sure, and I wondered if there were young children
in the family who were missing their little blonde
friend that looked like a miniature yellow lab. The
four of us piled into the VEPCO car for the trip
back to North Carolina and, I must say, DC was
seldom still ever again once he left that shelter.

At the time, I was renting a big two-story farmhouse on the edge of town, in the middle of a Black
Angus farm. I had a wonderful semi-Siamese cat
named Gabe whom I'll tell you about later, and
now, with DC, we were a three-person family. The
property was owned by the local beer distributor, a
Mr. Coppersmith. It never ceased to amaze me to see
a huge eighteen-wheeler drive out into the middle
of the pasture in the middle of the summer, see the
back doors open, and someone lead a humongous
bull or a new cow or two out of the refrigerated
truck.

When Mr. Coppersmith came out to his farm, he
was always accompanied by an old Black guy who
did all the work for him around the great old red

barn at the end of my driveway. Sometimes he'd leave the ol' fellow out there all day. Occasionally, I'd come home from work to find him sitting in the doorway of a little shed behind my house, waiting for his ride back to town and enjoying a few nips from a whiskey bottle he kept stashed there. I'd sit down in the grass and we'd have a nice visit. I wish I could remember his name. Usually though, when they were both there, he'd be doing one thing or another in the barn, and my landlord would–always!–be standing in front of the barn door, chain smoking. One afternoon I came home from work to that scene. I got out of the car and Mr. Coppersmith called me over.

"Did you know your dog likes tobacco?"

"What?"

"Watch this…" and he threw down a lit cigarette. Mind you, there were bits of straw littering the ground in front of the barn, especially where he was standing. DC watched him toss the butt, took a firm stance over it and barked at the cigarette, I guess until he built up a mouthful of saliva. Then that little fellow picked up the hot cigarette, chewed it a bit – and spat out the filter!

"He does this all day long!"

Like I said, DC was smart as a whip, and all I could figure was that he understood the danger of fire, and he intended to prevent another disaster like the one that, in a roundabout way, had given him to me.

DC moved with me when I went to southeastern North Carolina to live with Ellen Bryan. He loved living there! That dog rivaled the leap of a dolphin when he went up for a bounced tennis ball! Ellen's family owned a two-hundred-acre lake across the road from us, Bryan's Mill Pond. When Ellen and I took the johnboat out for a day of fishing, DC would swim behind us until we let him into the boat. Ellen didn't like for him to be in the boat, because he got so excited he whinnied like a pony, and Ellen thought he scared the fish away. One day she decided to teach him a lesson – I argued against it to no avail. She refused to let him into the boat. That poor guy swam and swam until he was so exhausted I was afraid he'd drown! The pond, which was surrounded on two sides by swampland, had a lot of downed cypress trees underwater and occasionally there would be a twig sticking up out of the water. I cried as I watched DC go from twig to twig, hang an elbow over one to rest a while, and then keep coming, still trying to get to us. Eventually he gave up and did make it back to shore. The tail that always curled up and over his butt drooped straight to the ground for the next three days.

Eventually, and sadly, he contracted heartworm disease. This was before many people had even heard of such a thing – I certainly hadn't. Even after the blindness it caused, he still had some good months. He remembered where he buried bones. He still enjoyed chewing the cover off golf balls and having the tightly wound rubber bands inside snap and pop him on the nose. Even so, I wished that I had not let our wonderful vet talk me out of letting him go earlier, because when he did die, it was not a easy death for him.

Gabe

"Gabe" was short for Gabriel, because he was such a little angel when I met him as a kitten, and he was my first feline love. The farmhouse was L-shaped, and the inside of the ell was a screened-in porch. The screen had a tear in a corner by one post; the dining room window opened onto the porch and I left it open a bit so that Gabe could come and go as he pleased. He was so good about greeting me when I got home from work, and if he wasn't there then, he certainly would show up before dark. But one night he didn't show up. Not by dark and not by the next morning. I knew in my gut something terrible had happened. I called my boss at VEPCO who, thank goodness, loved his cat as much as I loved mine, and through tears I told him I wouldn't be in that day – I had to find Gabe. To his credit, he told me to take however much time I needed and wished me luck. I will forever love him for that.

Later that afternoon I found Gabe lying in ankle-high grass between the house and the whiskey shed. I had looked all over, so he must've come that far in between my searching different areas. When I picked him up, I was horrified to find a large chunk of his side raw – a deep flesh wound! I always thought it looked as if a spinning car tire had clipped his side, but maybe a cow bit him; I'll never know. I had a great old vet who helped me nurse him back to health, and he and I had more precious time together.

But about a year later, I left to work in New York City and Mama and Daddy agreed to keep Gabe for me with them on our farm. Things went well for about a year, and then one day, Daddy found him lying in the garage, a tiny hole in his side and less than a teaspoonful of blood on the floor beside him. I didn't even get to say goodbye.

Bandit & Cleo

I don't recall when or how Bandit and Cleo arrived at our house at Bryan's Mill Pond. Bandit came first and didn't last very long. Ellen wasn't crazy about cats, and she wouldn't let him past the back porch; I felt lucky that she let me keep him. I loved that ol' tuxedo kitty, but in time something happened to him. He just went sort of nuts and favored biting whenever he had a chance. Then one day, he simply disappeared.

Cleo was a tiny cat, and what I call a "camouflage kitty" – she was every shade of brown and gold you can imagine, all mottled together, sort of like a clump of dried fall leaves. Coming home from town one day, I was going down the driveway that separated our house from the cornfield, and as I approached the back yard, I slowed down to watch Cleo. She was sitting at the edge of the field, looking at the ground. Then I saw a paw strike out at something. Then the other paw. What was she doing?

Was she messing with danger? I parked the GTO at the back door and sauntered out to the field. Perched in front of my cat was a tiny field mouse. I watched them stare at each other for a bit, then the mouse would charge at Cleo, she'd bat it away with her left paw. He'd roll off, stand up, shake his head, get back into position, stare again, and recharge. Whack! – right paw this time. They kept up this game as long as I could stand to watch and then, being human, as I was, I interfered. I said, "Cleo! You'd better leave that mouse alone – it's going to bite you!" She shot me a glance with a "meow!" which likely meant, "Mind your own damn business!" and the mouse, taking advantage of Cleo's inattention, ran up and *did* bite her on the leg! I learned an important lesson that day: let critters work it out for themselves. Just like Bandit, one day Cleo just wasn't there any more.

JB & Wicca & Magee

In 1978 I moved to Bowling Green, Ohio to study art history at Bowling Green State University. I had an apartment over TO's, a store across from campus. As I pulled into the parking lot one evening, two Bowling Green students met me and asked, "Is this your kitty?" They were holding a dirty, grubby-eyed, tiny, white kitten. No, it wasn't mine. Well, they wanted to know, could I please take it, because they lived on campus and could not have a pet. They had found it in the middle of the intersection, scared and shaking. I told them I'd take it and see if I could find the owner. That didn't happen. She cleaned herself up well that night, mostly while I went out and got a litter box and food for her. You know how it is—most pets name themselves as you observe their personalities, but in her case, no name seemed apparent for days.

The main business in the downstairs store was the printing of tee shirts, so lots of boxes were dumped in the big bin in the parking lot. The end of the week arrived and, with it, a spiffy idea. I hauled a bunch of boxes up to my apartment and with a box cutter and masking tape in hand, I proceeded to build a tower for the kitten: she could climb straight up through the tower that went from floor to ceiling, and she could poke her head out any number on holes on the sides of the boxes. She loved it! I'd come home from my grad classes, open the door (where I'd be facing her tower), and she would pop her head out of some hole and meow a hello to me! That cat never stopped entertaining me!

My closest friends in Bowling Green were Janet and Bucky; my favorite Scotch was J&B; and since she was a little jack-in-the-box – well, her name had to be JB! Speaking of Janet, I think JB loved her as much as she loved me. Janet would cradle her in her arms and they danced all around the living room floor. Another thing JB loved was ping-pong balls. Especially in the bathtub. And in the kitchen sink.

For the life of me, I don't remember how Wicca came to me. As you might surmise, she was a black cat, and she and JB did make a handsome pair! And while JB was in love with Janet, Janet's dog, Bones, was in love with Wicca. I don't even know how to put into words the relationship they shared, except to say that Bones swooned over that cat!

After living over TO's, we next lived in an apartment complex on the edge of town. I added an aquarium to the menagerie, and both cats loved to sit for hours watching the fish swim. Wicca was unmercifully possessive, demanding the best position, and if JB took Wicca's spot, she bopped her on the head.

JB slipped out of the apartment one winter day and was gone overnight. I was frantic! Not only was the parking lot busy, we were also very close to two busy streets. The next day, I found her snuggled behind a washing machine in the laundry room next door. She was as thankful to see me as I was to see her!

Both cats were young, so I thought I could train them to walk on leashes. I bought harnesses with matching leashes for them, a red set for Wic and purple for JB. We'd go out in style! When I got 'em outside, their bellies hit the sidewalk, and they wouldn't budge. Taking them for walks meant I carried a cat under each arm and we walked around the complex, colorful leashes dangling.

Later, JB, Wicca and I were sharing a larger apartment with my then-partner, Nancy, and our friend Elka. Elka loved the cats, but she didn't want them in her bedroom at night. Wicca, however, was a slick one: she'd hide under Elka's bed until after she turned her light out, and she'd try to join her. Nearly every night, we'd hear Elka's door open, hear her laugh, see Wic running down the hall, and hear

Elka's door close again. Sometimes she shifted her strategy and hid in the closet.

That cat did the damnedest thing – she would sit close in front of the refrigerator, which was over six feet high, stare at the top of it (maybe for a couple minutes), and then sail to the top of the fridge! As if she levitated! I watched her do that so many times – it was as if she imagined herself up there until her body simply joined her spirit. Then she'd sleep in a more than ample wooden bread bowl that was waiting there for her.

When she died, we buried her with some of her favorite things in my friend Dawn Glanz's back yard.

JB, however, stayed with me for many more years. One of those years was 1980 when I left Ohio and moved back to our farm in North Carolina. At the time, I was working in Charlotte's transportation department, making street signs. Two other women were on the crew, and one, who looked like a cliché of "a ninety-seven-pound weakling," was actually a professional wrestler. A ninety-*nine*-pound one. She and her partner, who was about two and a half times her size, lived in a large mobile home at the edge of some woods, and they invited JB and me to live with them so I'd be closer to work and not have to drive in from the farm every day. Sounded good. Sorry to say, their names escape me; I'll call them Wrestler and Roommate. They had a dog and a cat, and that cat had just had five kittens when we moved in with them. We all got along well enough, including all the critters. Then one day JB ran out the door. Once I discovered she was gone, I went out looking for her – and discovered that she was about twenty feet up a pine tree on its lowest limb, just staring down at me. I was horrified! And she was terrified. The fire department refused to help. I nailed plastic containers of cat food, of sardines, of anything I thought she might like to the tree, hoping to entice her to come down, all to no avail. She would not budge, no matter how much I called her, begged her, cussed her. I'm not talking "up a tree for an afternoon," I'm saying, lacking six hours, that cat was up that tree for seven days! Two of those days had her surviving a horrible rainstorm with lightning. And it got worse.

Wrestler and Roommate and I were regulars at meetings held by a woman who held "sessions"– I don't know what else to call them – at her house on Saturday nights. She was an ordained minister and a channel and fancied herself as a healer. That Saturday night was the end of JB's sixth day up the tree, and I told the group what had happened. Marian (how the hell can I remember her name and not the two women I was living with?) – anyway, Marian asked the group to join her in a visualization: to picture a spiral staircase going up the tree so that JB would not be fearful coming down. Well, now. Talk about a lesson in being specific about what you ask the Universe for. ... What Marian forgot to add was that the staircase should stop at that branch where JB was perched: I got home only to find her at least thirty-five feet up the tree after she had a freakin' staircase to climb! I called Marian to tell her what had happened.

The next day, she called me. She said that her son, who had overheard the conversation about JB, was going to help. He once worked for a tree-trimming company but had been injured badly in a fall and swore never to climb again. Now, however, he was willing to go up and rescue JB. Wow! I was to leave a pillow case between the front door and screen, along with a key. That young man dug out all his climbing gear, went to our place while we were at work, climbed the tree, slipped the pillow-case wrong-side-out over his arm, reached out and grabbed JB, slipped the case over her, tied it to his belt, and brought her safely down! I had my cat and he lost his fear of climbing!

JB had lost a little weight, but she was otherwise no worse for wear. She wasn't even dehydrated. The vet said she probably lived on rainwater and bugs on the limb.

JB kept moving with me – in her fifteen years we moved fifteen times! I swore that every time she saw me with a cardboard box, she had a cat-thought of, "Oh, crap, here we go again. ..." From that stint in North Carolina, we moved back to Bowling Green when I got a job in the School of Art at the university, and we lived there for ten more years. In 1991 I decided to leave the university, so our last move was from there to Tucson, Arizona.

My plan had been to move to Colorado and teach art with my dear friends Larry Hart and Steve Navarre, but that plan changed: Nancy decided she was also ready to move west and asked if we could move together. I told her that I'd never taken

269

a break from work, and I'd like not to work from when we moved in September until the first of the year. She suggested we get a Places Rated Almanac and pick a place to go for the winter and then each of us move somewhere after that. We chose Tucson, and moved here sight unseen. She and I co-owned a twenty-one-foot Sprinter motor home at the time. She, our good friend Nancy Eames, and JB traveled in it, while I drove the twenty-eight-foot diesel Ryder truck, jam-packed to the gills and with a trailer attached to the back that carried my Toyota Corolla wagon, also fully packed. All in all, I steered forty-five feet of possessions two thousand miles cross country. It was the first time in my life I truly lived up to the stereotype of "diesel dyke."

When JB and I moved to our second location in Tucson, we got a new roommate – Magee. Magee was a gorgeous black cat, sweet as pie, and we were back to the handsome yin-yang colors that JB and Wicca had shared some years before. One day I was lying on my bed with her, enjoying the Arizona sunshine pouring onto us through the clerestory windows. I noticed her color: each black hair was tipped in gold. I knew this had nothing to do with the sunshine – something was wrong. I took her to the vet and that sweet young thing was dying of kidney failure. She was barely a year old.

And that move – our fifteenth move together in fifteen years – was JB's last. She had begun shaking her head a lot and one day I came home from work and my apartment looked like a crime scene – every time she shook her head, blood flew from her right ear. Regina, our vet, determined she had an inoperable tumor behind her ear. Other than having been discovered in the street in Bowling Green fifteen years before and that crazy stint up the pine tree in Charlotte, JB had always been an indoor cat and in great health. By this time, Nancy was living with Helen, and Helen's green thumb meant they had a back yard that rivaled the Garden of Eden. I decided to let JB have one delicious romp in the grass and flowers before she had to leave this world. I took lots of photos of that precious white cat that day. Some people would call what happened weeks later with the next roll of film spooky – I called it a gift. I was taking more photos of Helen's flowers, in the same area I had photographed JB on her last day alive, and when I had that roll developed, there was a ghostly image of a white cat among the flowers, looking over her shoulder at me. I know, I know, it had to be the simple matter of a double exposure, didn't it? Well, I'm not so sure. ...

Boxer & Scooter

Ah, Boxer and Scooter. They are the two who crowd my furry memories with sheer delight! I bought this house across the street from Nancy and Helen in 1997. One day I made a choice that obliterated my deliberate decision to live here alone for a year: I went into a little nearby pet store just to see what was there. What was there was a large cage with two fur-balls inside – almost white, dark brown tips on every extension on the tiny bodies, and long sprigs of hair poking out everywhere. The sign said "Siamese." I asked the proprietor if they were long-haired Siamese. "Oh no – that's just baby hair." Siblings, the boy-cat had the brightest blue eyes I had ever seen! His sister was more of a runt; I was concerned she might not be well. Every animal I'd ever lived with was found or was a rescue, I'd never purchased one from a pet store, but I could not leave these kittens there, and I couldn't take just one sibling and leave the other behind. I handed over a hundred dollars and went home with a different commitment than the one to live alone for a year.

Names. I wasn't sure. I thought about naming Boy "Gabe" after the first, oh so sweet, Siamese I had lived with many years before, but I really thought he needed his own, original name; Girl, I thought maybe "Zoey." About a month later, I came home, entering through the garage and laundry room. When I turned to go down the hall toward the kitchen, Boy came running toward me, his first time to run to meet me. I burst out laughing! I remembered having seen Tony Danza during his boxing days out for a run, and this was like a kitten version of Tony Danza running toward me! I said, "BOXER! That's your name – Boxer!" A few days later I was in the bathroom, and – well, you know how cats have to accompany you to the toilet! – here comes Girl. She got to the doorway, flopped down on her side, and scooted to my feet. "SCOOTER! You're not a Zoey, you're a Scooter!" As cats should do, they had finally named themselves.

Scooter was a bit of a weakling in the beginning,

and I marveled at how Boxer taught her to play, helping her build her strength. He was a good teacher, a good brother. As they grew, Scooter became a tiny bit "chunky," not fat, but certainly "thicker" than Boxer's svelte self. And yes, Mr. Proprietor, they *were* long-haired Siamese. I had shared life with some beautiful critters, but these two were spectacular! And it turned out that they had personalities unsurpassed by all the others. They loved each other, clearly; they were so cute sleeping together in their favorite chair. But when it came to me, Boxer deferred space and time to Scooter. For the years that I thought he just didn't care for me as much as Scooter did, I was to learn later that he was just being a gentleman cat. For instance, while Scooter slept on top of me, Boxer slept on the lower far corner of the bed.

Scooter was my OCD kitty: before going to sleep at night, she *had* to lick each one of my fingertips. If she missed one, she'd return to it. Every single night. She and Boxer both loved to travel cross-country with me in my Winnebago. Scooter insisted on claiming the passenger seat, relegating Boxer to find himself a spot on the bed above my head. Scooter died in 2008 during her birthday month of May. She had brought me immeasurable pleasure along with a fair share of clingy aggravation for eleven years. It was a sad day when she died – on our way to the vet.

I'll tell you more about Boxer later. ...

Cass

In my experience, I think black and white cats are the most affectionate. Two came to live with me in this house. The first was a stray that I discovered sleeping under my RV when I opened the side door to the garage one day. I put food and water out for him, not knowing whether he had a home to go to or not. The next day, he was still here. And the next. I let him into the garage with me while I was working out there; I sat down and he jumped into my lap; he even let me clip the tips of his nails.

I had planned to be away for a few days, and my best friend, Sandy, was going to come over to take care of Boxer and Scooter; I told her about the visitor and asked her to check on him. Sure enough, and much to my surprise, he was still here when I returned. However, a few days later, he disappeared for three days. When he came back, he was a mess! He was dirty and all his nails were ground down to nubs! Damn! What had happened to him? I knew it was time to give him a real home, so I took him to the vet to make sure he was healthy enough to be with Boxer and Scooter. She saw his dirty sides – like soot – and his worn-down nails, and said, "He literally clawed his way out of some place to get back to you." What a little lover he was! I decided to name him Cassanova – Cass for short.

The three cats got along fine, no problems even between the two males in the house, which amazed me. I'm not remembering how long he was here – maybe two years? – and one afternoon he was sleeping by the sliding glass doors in the den. As the day lengthened and cooled, I went over to close the door, and asked Cass to move since his paw was in the way. He didn't budge. I nudged him with my toe, and he still didn't move. Cass simply had lain down and died. I ordered a necropsy and learned that he apparently had a congenital heart problem. He was a real sweetheart –and although I don't know what his life had been like before he came here, I do hope I gave him as much love as he gave to me. He was special.

Tess

Convoluted turns led me to another little black-and-white already named Tess. Her elderly human had died, and the daughter who lived in Alaska was down here taking care of things and wanted to find homes for her mother's two cats. Eventually, against my better judgment, I agreed to take Tess. She, too, was a sweet, loving cat, but, oh god, did she ever have more than her share of problems. Scooter and Cass were already gone, so she and Boxer were the only cats here. Boxer always got along with every-body – people, dogs, even Cass coming in as a male stranger – but he did not like Tess and she was terrified of him. They were always fighting; I had yet to learn what was happening to me health-wise and was living with screaming pain (literally!) as paralysis was setting in, so I could not care for her as I should. She ended up being passed along to two other friends, and I am not remembering what happened to her in the end. All I know for sure is that I should've listened to my gut instincts.

Boxer Stands Alone

I wondered how Boxer would adjust to Scooter's absence after she died. I'm sure he missed her presence but, I tell you, this is when he began to reveal his true self. We became very close, and I talked to him a lot. He looked at me as if he understood. No matter where I was in the house, if I called his name, he came running. I didn't have to call "Kitty, kitty!" just "Boxer!" or "Boxer?" Not long after Scooter died, I was diagnosed with diabetes and sleep apnea. Thank goodness, after losing some weight, sleep apnea is no longer a problem, but back then the first sleep test showed that I was waking up over six hundred times a night! Can you imagine? So you won't be surprised to hear that I was forever falling asleep on the toilet or at the computer. I mean deep sleep! I called those episodes little mini comas. Sometimes I'd wake up only when my forehead hit the keyboard! It was during that time that I realized that Boxer had become my "helper cat." He would climb on the back of my chair, tap me on the back, and wake me. He'd sense I was in trouble in the bathroom and come in there and meow long enough to wake me. In 2012 when I became partially paralyzed and was spending a lot of time in bed, unable to see what was happening outside, he'd run into the bedroom with eager meowing; when I moved to my wheelchair to go to the bathroom and passed the back door, I could see that it was raining. That's how I learned his language for rain. Nearly all the time that I was in bed, he was by my side, holding "hands" with me. Moving through the house in my wheelchair, I always carry my iPad on my lap. Boxer sat on it, riding with me. I called him my hood ornament.

In the summer of 2015, he began slowing down and losing weight. He had cancer. Time came for the Big Decision that none of us wants to make, but I would not make him live just for me. He and I had a talk. Believe that. My friends Sandy Treadwell and Pat Keeler took us to the vet on November 2. Boxer and I butted heads, held hands, and I knew he was ready and willing – and thankful – to go. He was almost nineteen years old when he died. Boxer was the most devoted creature I have ever known. No offense to the human ones, but I must say he was also the best roommate I ever had. Over a year later, I still occasionally "see" him out of the corner of my eye, and Facebook Memories that pop up continuously remind me of the sweet photos I posted of him. I swear, he had more friends on Facebook than I do! My life was blessed beyond belief by the love of that cat. I wish everyone could have such a friend as he was to me.

SyndiLou

Joanne Ferguson lives directly across the street from me. Joanne is retired Army, a cop at Tucson International Airport, one of the smartest people

I know, someone who can do just about anything. Not only is she my tech-guru, she has rescued me with her friendship. She has also rescues animals. I've lost count of how many little lost souls she has found in the neighborhood and at the airport, and her "detective" skills make her very good at finding owners who have lost their pets – or finding new homes for ones that have simply been abandoned.

She herself lives with a crowd of critters: two mini-pincers, Rocko and Bruno; Allie, the sweetest pit bull you'd ever come to love; and two Siamese cats, Ace and Badger. Ace had lived in a parking lot at the airport for a few years. When Joanne learned he was there, she made sure he had food and water every day. After two years of that, he let her know in no uncertain terms that he was adopting her, and she brought him home. He insisted on being able to go outside, so she installed a cat door for him to go from the house to the garage, and another cat door in the garage door so he could get outside. A few years ago, that little guy had quite an adventure. He disappeared, and ten months later, Joanne got a call from an animal shelter in Wisconsin, of all places – 2,000 miles away: someone had left Ace in a crate at their front door, no note, and because she is an avid believer in microchips, they knew to notify her that they had her cat. Southwest Airlines flew him home. TV cameras were there, as well as a horde of Joanne's and Ace's mutual fans and friends to cele-brate his arrival. Needless to say, Ace no longer has as much interest in being an outdoor cat. He does have a cat condo that he can get to that mimics being "outdoors," but mostly he stays inside and snuggles up to his pit bull buddy.

There had been a third Siamese member of the household but since the other cats mistreated her, she had to stay in a room by herself. After Boxer died, Joanne approached me, wanting to know if I would take Syndi. I said no, because I wanted Boxer to be my final Siamese memory, and I wanted my next cat to be black. Unable to drive to and roam through shelters to see which cat and I might "click," I pored through shelter websites. Nobody stood out.

Joanne asked again. And again. Finally, I said, "Let me see a photo." She bore no resemblance to Boxer – he was very light, she a dark seal brown. "Well, bring her over and we'll see what she thinks. ..." She ran back across the street and fetched the cat. Syndi was a bit stand-offish but didn't run and hide; that was a decent sign, I figured. I agreed to have her spend the night, so Joanne ran home again and brought her food and litter pan.

The next day, she brought her tower.

That was December 6, 2015 and we've been housemates ever since. Seemed to me she needed a Southern name, so she became SyndiLou. She definitely has two human moms. While she and I got off to a slow start, we've made a lot of progress in our fifteen months together and have become good companions. She is one smart cookie! I have watched her vocabulary grow – for example, she understands the sentence that begins "I gotta go..." which lets her know she has to get off my bed-lap in a hurry because I'm about to get up to go to the bathroom. I ask her to wait for me because I'll be back in bed soon, and she usually does. We also share some favorite TV shows.

So – here I am, now seventy-four years old and living with my sixteenth furry buddy, SyndiLou Ferguson Aldridge. Thank you, Joanne.

~February 25, 2017~

Chapter 46

Biggest Compliment

Some of you know I used to be a sign painter –
mostly in the '70s. I had a sign shop in Lumberton,
North Carolina back then. When I went into
business I didn't even have the sense to check the
Yellow Pages and find out I was going to be the
seventh sign painter in a town of about thirty thousand people. Good I was too dumb to check, for I
might've been discouraged right out of existence as
a sign painter!

Well, there was one old man in town, in his seventies,
who did the most gorgeous lettering! I could always
recognize his work from everyone else's. One day
I called him to see if I could go meet him in his
working garage; he greeted me graciously. I told him
I just wanted to let him know how much I admired
his work and wished I could be half as skilled as
he was, I knew I would be no competition for him,
but I just wanted to meet him. He said he had seen
some vans I had lettered for the fire department with
gold paint (kind of a fake gold-leaf paint – liquid
paint with actual gold flecks in it – same paint used
on North Carolina State Highway Patrol cars) and

that I did "very good work." Wow.

But the BIGGEST compliment was to come from him later. ... While working in my shop one day the phone rang. It was my sign-painting idol. He said, "Do you know how to do gold leaf?"

"No."

"Well, if you want to learn be down at the bank at 7 a.m. tomorrow and I'll teach you."

JEEZ! You may not have a clue what a process it is to do gold leaf lettering. It is an incredible skill, one that even requires taking the weather into account while one does it, and a process that has many steps, none of them obvious to the layperson as the finished product is observed, even passed by without a thought about how that beauty came to be. And it is a technique that is apprenticed – not something anyone could easily learn from a book. Trust me. You tape your "cartoon" (pattern) on the outside of the window. On the inside, you brush on sizing, in the shape of the letters, sizing you've concocted from gelatin capsules. Remember, you're lettering backwards. Then you lay the gold leaf onto the sizing using a special brush for "lifting/laying" – actually, you rub that brush across your hair to build up some static electricity so that the brush WILL pick up the leaf from the "book" that it is in, each page (leaf) separated by thin pieces of paper, and from a leaf that you've scored with your thumbnail to the desired size you need to pick up. Then you burnish the gold with a cotton ball and trim it into the shape of the letter using a single-edged razor blade. Cutting curved edges of letters are loads of fun (not!). Then you use a quill lettering brush (none better than Langnickel brushes) to paint the letters, covering the leaf with Japan black. After that dries – hours pass – you go back to the job site and letter again, this time with 1-Shot Lettering Black, not only in the shape of the letter but larger enough that each letter has an even outline all around it. It ain't easy, folks.

Believe me, I showed up! He explained to me how gold leaf is made: it starts out with a piece of gold about the size of a silver dollar, and that piece is hammered, hammered, hammered until a sheet is formed that will "fill an eight-foot by eight-foot room," he said.

And you know what else this Michelangelo of signs said to me? He said, "I am the only gold leaf painter in these parts. In fact, for years sign painters from a hundred miles around have begged me to teach them, and I won't. Because I don't like their work. But I've been watching you and I do like yours, so I wanted to teach you."

That, my friends, I have always considered the greatest professional compliment I have ever received.

~March 6, 2017~

Chapter 47

Dreaming

Sleep is a strange beast. Or mine is, at least. Lately, anyway.

Because of my health condition, I usually sleep no more than two hours at a time. On the rare occasion that I manage four hours – well, that's my idea of luxury. A year or so ago I started noticing my dreams were changing; so was their style. My dreams have always been in living color, and they usually contain people, people with whom I am having a conversation. Often, of late, those people are dead. I don't exactly hear their voices; I just know what they are saying. My end of the conversation, however, is a different story: I am speaking. Out loud. I am still asleep (to some degree), but I hear my own voice, feel my mouth moving – I am actually talking. I am also conscious of how strange all of this is while it's happening. Is that what's called "lucid dreaming"? I should look into that.

I especially like the dead-people dreams; there is no doubt in my mind that they are visiting me. I do believe I have spent more meaningful time with my mama in this way than I ever did in real life. Well, "live" life. Who's to say which is more real? The point is, Mama and I didn't talk a whole lot when she was alive. Oh, we spent a lot of time together; we just didn't have conversation very much. I never knew her personal feelings about things – religious beliefs, politics, such stuff as that. I wish I had.

I don't know if you think what I just told you is weird, but if you don't think this next bit is weird – well, you are weirder than I am. Once in a while, I'm not aware of any dream activity, but I say something, something clearly directed at someone, I just have no idea who it is. I hear myself speaking, and I see what I am saying. What does it look like? The words are in a bold font, not sure which one, and they are housed in a speech bubble. You know, like in a cartoon: the little cloud-bubble with a tail pointing to the head of whoever is talking. The more significant the statement, the bigger the bubble and the bigger and bolder the font. Of course, none of it is ever *actually* significant, certainly not enough so that I remember my words when I wake. And I wake immediately after seeing the bubble. Sort of like the bubble bursts and I'm back here. That happened once this morning.

After returning to sleep, I had one of those other dreams. I have never dreamed about my editor before, but she was the star of this one. Linda Lauby is brilliant, not only with her editing skills, but her writing, her photography, her art, her business. As if those characteristics aren't enough reasons for her to be someone I'd like, she's also funny and kind and good to me. Neither does it hurt that she lives in one of my favorite places on the planet, the Outer Banks of North Carolina, and that she loves her dogs. She's never said, and neither has Paul, so far as I know, but I suspect she loves them as much as she loves him, and he's her husband.

So in this dream, we've been spending time together (mind you, we've never met in person, I'm sorry to say), and I'm not sure what all had been happening, but in the end she's telling me she was very nervous about a speech she had to give. I asked why – she deals with people all the time, and I couldn't imagine speaking to a group of people would be hard for her. So I assumed the "group" must've been a huge crowd, like an auditorium full of people.

"How many people were there?"

"Oh, at least a hundred!"

Well, that seems like nothing, I thought. I mean, I don't know jack-shit compared to Linda with all her talents and travels and experiences, and I've spoken to as many as eight hundred at a time. What I said to her next, so far as I know, has no basis in fact – except that she is beautiful enough for it to be true; if I'm wrong, she can edit me. I said, "But Linda! You were in a Miss America contest – you were in front of thousands of people!"

She said, "But that was just tap dancing!"

And I woke up.

~April 14, 2017~

Editor's note: Nope, I've never been in a Miss America contest and furthermore, I am seriously dancing-impaired. I'd rather have a rat in my mouth.

Chapter 48

How Come Tucson?

When I was growing up in North Carolina, folks said of one of our tourist attractions, "All roads lead to Chimney Rock." All my roads have led to Tucson.

I wasn't exactly a "professional student," but I did go to college three times. First, directly out of high school in 1960, I attended what was then East Carolina College, formerly East Carolina Teachers College, then East Carolina College, later to be called East Carolina University, and still later, the University of North Carolina-Greenville.

My whole life, since old enough to hold a pencil to paper, I had loved to draw. My high school didn't offer art classes, however, and I thought I couldn't major in art in college without some background training. My parents, bless 'em, did pay for me to take the correspondence course from Art Instruction, Inc., but that certainly didn't seem to me to be suitable enough to count as serious training. That home study course focusing on cartooning and illustration was based in Minneapolis, and their ads were everywhere – from inside magazines to inside matchbook covers – each famous with the line, "Draw me!" A student received weekly lessons, would fulfill the assignment, send it back to the instructor in charge of that lesson, and wait for him (I think it was always a "him") to return a critique. Can't say it really did much more for me than adding yet more homework to my already busy high school senior year. Well, one other thing it did give me was a sincere appreciation that my parents recognized some talent that I had and were willing to spend their good money supporting my interests. That was no small thing, 'cause Daddy was tight as a tick with his money.

So, instead of art, I chose to major in home economics. If you could see inside my house nowadays, you'd swear I forged my diploma. Home economics was touted as "the career with a thousand and one job titles," and in time that curriculum did provide me with a number of job opportunities that I enjoyed to varying degrees, but I kept telling myself that some day I'd go back to school for art. And that I did.

In 1972 I began classes at Pembroke State University in Pembroke, North Carolina. PSU had been established in 1887 as the first teachers school for Indians in North Carolina. It, too, went through many name changes – first from Croatan Normal School to Indian Normal School of Robeson County, to the Cherokee Indian Normal School of Robeson County. In 1954 the school began allowing anyone, regardless of race, to apply, and attendance bounded.

I should add here that Pembroke, the town – well,

it wasn't exactly a "town," more an area of Robeson County – was primarily Indian, Lumbee Indian. The Lumbees are a people who have never been able to prove their origins. One theory, and the one I find most believable, dates back to the late sixteenth century when Sir Walter Raleigh established an English Colony in what is now Manteo, North Carolina. During the second winter, a very rough one, ships had returned to England for supplies; when they came back to their "new world," they found the colony deserted. On a nearby tree they found the letters "CRO" carved, the full word "CROATOAN" carved into a fence post, and many people have interpreted those finds to mean that the settlers, who had made friends with the local Croatan Indians, had gone inland with them in order to survive. Supporting that theory is the fact to this day – or at least to the time I lived in the area – many of the Lumbee Indians have blue eyes and speak with an English brogue. But, as I said, they can't even prove, to the satisfaction of the American government, that they are Indian; therefore, they were never given ("given" – ha!) reservation rights or any recognition of any kind. Most of the residents of the area lived in poverty, and the school provided an opportunity for the young ones to improve their lot in life.

When I began my studies in 1972, that's the year it became known as Pembroke State University. In 1996, along with all state-supported schools in North Carolina, it took on the name of the greater system, followed by a hyphen and the name of its location, so it is now the University of North Carolina-Pembroke. Because my earlier general education credits transferred from East Carolina, I was able to take nothing but art classes and finished a bachelor's degree in art education in two years. It was heaven!

I was living with Ellen Bryan back then outside Lumberton and a twenty-eight mile commute to campus. Ellen taught physical education there and coached the women's volleyball team. When the school was building a brand-spankin' new fancy gymnasium, somebody forgot to include in their million-dollar budget any plans for what needed to be painted on the gym floor – the image of the sports mascot (a brave's head) and the team's name in front of each set of bleachers. The school's athletic director put two and two together as cheaply as he could, and decided since I lived with one of his faculty members and I was an art major, I would do the job for nothing. I didn't. I mean, I did the job, but not for nothing. Not sure what I charged him, but four hundred dollars sticks in my mind – and that was like a freebie: I gave them a brand new, strong, handsome brave's head, designed from scratch, painted it in a six-foot-circle center court, and lettered "BRAVES" facing each sideline. While that might not have been much to charge for the project, "payment" continued: the financial officer of the school saw my work and liked it; he hired me to letter signs for the tennis courts. Then to letter campus trucks. In fact, he kept giving me enough work that it paid for my senior year there.

What's more, it inspired me: I knew I really didn't want to teach again, so I decided to open a sign

shop in Lumberton, the town between Pembroke
and where Ellen and I lived out in the country,
and that was some of the most interesting work I
ever did. I designed letterheads, logos, and business
cards for clients. I lettered everything from small,
personalized license plates for the front of cars
to forty-foot wide signs on the side of a building.
I lettered fleets of eighteen-wheelers and school
buses and race cars (including climbing on the roof
to paint giant numbers). I designed billboards for
3M: they took my color drawings, fed them into a
new-fangled computerized machine, and out came
a vinyl product that they stretched onto their giant
billboards that cluttered the highways. I met a lot of
interesting people I would not have known otherwise, including the other sign painters in town, in
particular the old guy I told you about who chose
me to teach gold leaf lettering instead of the dozens
of painters from miles around who had begged him
to teach them. I never asked; he called and offered
because, he said, he liked my work. What an honor.

I did well with the shop. I didn't pay myself a salary,
but I had money to buy a steak any time I wanted
one – and I bought a new GTO. After three years,
I closed the shop to move home while Mama was
dying of cancer. Later, I moved back to Ellen's,
bought an old trailer that had been used as an office
at a construction site, and used it as my sign shop on
her property. I kept my skills honed for quite a few
years, but like any skill and any muscle, if you don't
use it, you lose it. Now, if anyone asks me to letter
anything, my palms begin to sweat. I'm no longer
good at it, but I still have my treasured Langnickel

quill brushes, all oiled and safely stored – just in case.

Eventually, I needed to "get away." I needed to restart my life. The only solution I could come up with was grad school, so I ended up at Bowling Green State University in northwest Ohio to work toward a master's degree in art history. Truth be told, I didn't go there with a goal: I just needed a respectable adult cop-out. It turned out to be one of the most important moves of my life; I met some wonderful people with whom I've shared friendships for almost forty years, each one of them a treasure. I spent two years in grad classes, returned to North Carolina for ten difficult months, then went back to Bowling Green to run the Art Resource Center in the School of Art and teach a few beginning art/ art history classes for non-majors. After eight years in the ARC, I took a job as assistant director in the Women's Studies Program. After three years of that, I was fried. Really burnt to a crisp! In 1991 the day came that I was supposed to sign my contract for the next year.

So there I was, sitting at my desk in Women's Studies, needing to sign my contract for the next year and my hand would not pick up the pen! I knew if I continued to work at the university, it would kill me. It wasn't the work required by the job description, it was something I could not have expected. Back then there were no "safe houses" for abused women, nowhere for women to go who needed advice and emotional support. So for miles around, those women would search phone books and who knows what other sources (few people had computers then), and they would see our Women's Studies Program listed and come to my office to talk about the horrible things they were enduring, usually with a terribly abusive husband. Listening to them was heartbreaking and scary and emotionally draining for me. Three years of it took its toll.

Back to the contract: I sat frozen in my seat, and I heard a booming voice in my head: "Pull out your retirement and haul ass!" Well, I am paraphrasing a bit, but the message was clear: LEAVE!

Now I have to backtrack a minute, back to Pembroke. ... One of my instructors was a tiny little man named John Flynn. Interesting fellow. I'm sorry I lost track of him after he left Pembroke. He painted the most incredible landscapes – with crayons, no less! He also designed stage sets. I don't think he ever produced them; I think he was just interested in opera and liked to imagine how the story should be set. I was older than most of the students, thirty years old, and that meant John and I were fairly close in age. One day in class, and right of the blue, he asked me, "Have you ever been to the Southwest?" I said I had not, and he said, "Well, don't go, because if you do, you will never want to come back."

Almost twenty years after John said that to me, Nancy Dillon and I were living together in Bowling Green. We decided to take a vacation to New Mexico, Arizona, and Colorado, so we headed out in her trusty little Subaru. We went to Taos, Santa Fe, then across to Phoenix, over to the quaint town of Prescott, magical Sedona, and up to the Grand Canyon. We didn't go to the southern halves of Arizona and New Mexico. We backtracked to get one more delicious taste of Taos and then went to Colorado for a sweet visit with Larry Hart and Steve Navarre, who had been students at Bowling Green.

But what I need to tell you about is what happened in Sedona. At that time, cars could drive down to the creek that is a part of the famous view of Cathedral Rock. We parked the car, carried our picnic and bamboo mats down to the water's edge, had our lunch, and then settled in for a peaceful rest. I was wearing a necklace that had a clear, tricolor octahedron hanging on the chain. In case you don't know what that looks like, imagine two pyramids together, base against base. The octahedron's top section was a light amethyst color; the middle, clear; the bottom third, a light topaz color. I took the necklace from around my neck and began to use it as a pendulum, asking a lot of questions for which I wanted answers, just yes-no answers. After a while, instead of putting the necklace back on, I dropped it into the pocket of my denim shirt, and I took a nap.

Soon, Nancy and I were back on the road, ready to head back to Taos. I remembered the necklace and pulled it from my pocket. As I started to put it on, I noticed a sparkle. Inside the central transparent section of the stone, believe it or not, was a check mark – a check mark made of tiny gold flecks! I laughed out loud! One of the questions I had asked the pendulum was, "Will I ever be able to move out here?" The pendulum swung a "yes," but I didn't believe it – I had thought, *Yeah – right! Pffftt!* I showed Nancy what I was seeing, and I said, "When the time is right, the money will be available." I was certain of the message. So a few years later "The Voice" said to me, "Take out your retirement. ..." I knew the time had come.

By that time, Nancy and I weren't living together as partners, but we were still friends. I told her I was going to leave, and she said she was finally ready to go, too. We decided to move together – somewhere – we just weren't sure where. We bought a **Places Rated Almanac**, studied demographics, and chose Tucson. We would move there for the winter and in the spring each of us would decide where we'd go next. As it turned out, we both loved Tucson so much that twenty-six years later we are both still here, and still friends.

~May 5, 2017~

Chapter 49

Winding Down

If you think about it, it might seem silly, even ridiculous, that I have been recording these memories from almost fifteen years ago, but there are reasons for the span of time.

While I still deal with residual effects, back then there were serious problems stemming from having received a TBI, a traumatic brain injury. It happened on May 5, 1997. I was on a four-lane street waiting for a car to exit a parking lot so I could turn into it. A guy in a pickup truck, hurrying home for lunch and going at least 45 miles per hour, plowed into the back of my RAV4 as I sat dead still in the street. My head bounced against the headrest and I was out cold. I don't know how long I was unconscious, but after a while, eyes still shut, I was aware of someone shaking my shoulder and repeating, "Are you okay? Are you okay?" over and over and over. I finally came to enough to say to him, "I don't know. All I *do* know is that I am royally pissed!" My car was one year old – to the day. We both pulled into the parking lot and he claimed to go into the store to call the police; when I saw two police cars go down the street without stopping, I realized that he had done no such thing. I took out my cell phone, called my insurance agent and then the police. Eventually they arrived and ticketed the other driver. It never occurred to me that I should've gone to an emergency room (though it probably would've done no good because, especially then, few doctors were very knowledgeable of concussions). I did go to my chiropractor and learned that I had received a whiplash. As time went on, I also learned a whiplash is a serious matter. There are a lot of rear-end collisions in and around Tucson, and frequently a reporter on scene will say, "No serious injuries – just a few people with whiplashes," and I want to smack 'em! Not serious, my ass!

Medically, it was called a "mild" TBI. Don't let *anyone* ever tell you there *is* such a thing as a mild TBI. Ask any one of my dozen-plus friends who live with one. Focus was a major problem – or *lack* of the ability to focus, I should say. Well, actually, it was a bit more complicated than that: I either could not focus at all *or* I would be super focused, as in almost manic-mode to carry out some task. A TBI brings fatigue, depression, and learning a lot of new coping skills. Trouble is, for a while – in my case, several years for some of the issues – one might not even recognize what is haywire. Case in point: for a long time after the wreck and injury, I had a lot of trouble typing. Months later I realized I had to correct tons of typos with every email I was writing. Then it took even longer to realize there was a pattern to the errors. What I intended to type with my right ring finger, for example an "o," ended up being a "w." Not just that finger, but others, too. My wires were so crossed that my brain was telling the wrong hand to do what I meant for the other to do. Talk about frustrating! And even to this day, now twenty-one years after the wreck, if I get very tired, my fingers again seem to forget which hand they are on.

Recently, when I decided I wanted the last entry in this little book to be about what my life is like now, I thought it would be a good opportunity to educate people about TBI, what it's like to live with an injured brain *and* what it's like to live with a person who has one. But to tell you the truth, folks, I am just too tired to do it. I will suggest to you, never underestimate a bang on the head, your own or anyone else's. And for heaven's sake, if you have kids or grandkids, *please* do all you can to protect their noggins. And that includes keeping them from playing sports that, in all likelihood, *will* result in concussion. Think about it: you'll know which sports they are. And read. Read all you can about concussions and their aftermath. A head cannot be struck with any appreciable force without that juicy brain bouncing against the inside of the skull. Helmets are good for keeping a skull from cracking, but they don't stop that bouncing brain. Remember that. Please.

I have no smooth segue for this, so I'll just say I'm remembering as a teen seeing the beautiful actress Polly Bergen being interviewed on TV. She said she loved to sleep naked. My mama was appalled! Pragmatist that she was, she said, "What would she do if her house caught on fire and she had to run outside?" I said I reckoned she would wrap a sheet around herself and go. Years after that I learned it *does* feel best to sleep naked. Furthermore, it feels pretty fine to do anything and everything around the house "stark nekkid." Living alone, I could do that and not expose anyone within seeing distance to the saggy imagery I carried around with me. That is, until February 17, 2012.

I had been writing and went to the kitchen to retrieve some salsa and chips to munch on while I worked at the computer. Just as I turned the corner from the kitchen to walk the short hallway to my desk, I fell. I still cannot believe that jar of salsa did not break! I'm thankful I didn't end up falling onto broken glass, and I'm even more thankful I didn't break any bones. I discovered I could not stand up. (Yeah, that would be your cue to mock me with, "Help! I've fallen and I can't get up!") I crawled the twenty or so feet to my desk. There was an ottoman underneath the desk where I propped my feet while I worked; I pulled it out and draped my nakedness over it, thinking it would give me something to hold onto while I tried again, if not to stand, somehow to lift myself into my chair. No such luck, Sherlock.

I managed to reach my cell phone and I called my best friend, who lived about three miles away. Sandy suggested that I call my neighbors across the street and have them come over while she drove here. Soon, Sandy, Joanne and Donna were here, all three of them trying to get my naked ass off the floor and into my chair. I was dead weight. The only thing they could do was to call 911 and manage to get some clothes on me before the EMT guys arrived. It took three of those burly boys to get me up and onto a stretcher. It was my first ride in an ambulance. No one at the hospital could figure out what was wrong, and they eventually sent me home with one of those fancy walkers, the kind with four wheels, a seat, and handbrakes.

Exactly one month later, on March 17, I was using the walker to go to the bathroom and the walker got away from me – down I went. This time, with Joanne and Donna helping me, I was able to get up. Again, nothing broken. Whew! But by this time, I was experiencing a lot of pain. A LOT! Screaming pain. It had started in late 2011 but now it was excruciating. It had begun in my left buttock and thigh and soon claimed my right thigh.

Then – would you believe? – on *April* 17 I fell again, again on the way to the bathroom. Really sore, but nothing broken. However, after three falls in exactly two months, it was time to find *someone* who could tell me what the hell was going on! I was in the hospital for enough days to qualify to go to rehab afterward, but even after scans, MRIs, spinal taps, you name it, there was still no diagnosis for why I was unable to walk normally and for why I was in such ungodly pain. They were giving me morphine for the pain. Because of no diagnosis, some of the re-hab work was more harmful than helpful. I did come home from rehab with a manual wheelchair.

My primary care physician, Dr. Martha Miller, sent me to a neurologist because she thought she knew what was wrong. As it turned out, she had another patient with similar symptoms who had been diagnosed with lumbosacral plexopathy, or LSP. Sure enough, Dr. Horak (the neurologist) ordered still more tests – including nerve tests – and in June gave me the diagnosis; Martha had been right. The bundle of nerves at the base of the spine just went whacko and pretty much stopped working as they were supposed to, resulting in partial paralysis of my legs.

Dr. Horak told me it is a very rare disease. At that time, .003 percent – that's only three-thousandths of one percent! – of the American population had it. And that explains why virtually no research has been done on it: the drug companies won't make any money off of us. However, she was encouraging: she said that most cases resolve themselves within six to twelve months.

Well, six months came and went. Twelve months came and went. Twenty-four months, and she was saying, "Well, you've got a really stubborn case. ..." Now, as I write this, it's been eight months, and with additional complications: for example, the nerves also affect the bladder, so Depends and Poise Pads have become my allies. My ankles are barely flexible, and my toes are curling downward. There is rarely any let-up from pain, although it is pretty much limited to my lower legs and feet. Tylenol with codeine gets me through the days and nights. But speaking of days and nights, those designations no longer have any meaning for me: I have to pee about every two hours, so it's rare that I even get as much as three hours of sleep at a time, so I sleep when I can, any time of day or night, and seldom feel rested.

Dr. Horak had also said LSP comes on suddenly and usually leaves suddenly. But I was able to realize, finally, that it had sneaked up on me. For at least a year before the series of falls, I was weary. I had trouble walking up steps – if there was no rail to hold onto, I had to go up on all fours, my hands flat on an upper step and my feet on a lower one, climbing the steps like an animal, and then sit to come down, dropping my butt to each lower step. I was driving my friend Pat to physical therapy twice a week then, and eventually I was just too tired to go inside to wait for her; I just waited in the car. You wonder why I didn't get help sooner? I couldn't put it all together. Remember the TBI? Clear thinking was not a given.

Four years ago, Dr. Horak prescribed a power wheelchair for me. It cost more than the GTO I bought in 1965. A friend who requested to remain anonymous paid the copay for me, bless her heart, and another friend bought the chair lift for the back of my car. This chair has been a lifesaver in many ways. So much easier to get around in the house and I can even "st-roll" the two-plus miles to the drug store and grocery store. Not easy to do and it creates more leg pain, but it does mean I can exercise a wee modicum of independence some days and get out of the house. Sandy decorated it with an orange worker's vest over the back of the chair and attached a tall orange flag so that, hopefully, no crazy Tucson driver will hit me. I must tell you though, the worst thing about this disease is that I am no longer able to drive, the biggest measure of independence.

So – what? Well, the "what" is that I have had to learn to find the "gift" in this life change. I don't mind telling you, that doesn't come easily some days.

I had always liked to help others, now I had to learn to ask for help. And, pretty much, the only thing I now have to give to others is my love and gratitude. I have friends who are undoubtedly the best in the world – the nearest are Joanne Ferguson, across the street, and Sandy Treadwell, about three miles away. I promise you, I could not manage without them. Do you know what a gift it is to answer the phone and hear, "I'm at the grocery store; what do you need?" And, "I'm coming over tomorrow to change your bed linens." Or, "Would you like to go to a movie this week?" And Joanne not only carries out my recycling and trash for me every Monday night, but every week for over five years she has rolled the bins to the street and back. She comes over to visit nearly every night. Friend-wise, I am a most fortunate creature.

I've learned that I am annoyed to hell and back by people who spout platitudes like "Just be happy!" I get into arguments with people who insist I can just "change my attitude." Maybe some people can do that, but I can't. And "living in the moment" has taken on a whole new meaning for me. I *do* live in the moment: it's just that some moments I'm pleasant and fun and even happy to a degree, but give me a minute and I might be royally pissed about life in general. And do you know what? I've learned that *that* is okay. It's just fine, in fact. It's *life*. I've learned to recognize the Light in me and I've learned to accept the Dark side, too. Actually, I think we should all do that. I'm thankful to see all parts of me, even though I don't always like what I'm looking at.

I've also learned that chronic pain is all consuming: it

demands one's awareness, it insists on attention. So, to turn my mind toward writing, or toward trying to reclaim apparently lost painting and drawing skills, or to tackle what used to be normal, everyday chores – well, most of the time those things are impossible.

I've learned that most people do have some kind of crap in their lives that they are dealing with. It may be a physical condition we can spot, but possibly it's what is invisible to others that causes them the most grief. When someone is driving me somewhere, I look at people in other cars and wonder what their lives are like, and I send them love-vibes. When someone's driving too fast, I wonder if they need to get to someone they love who is in trouble. I try to give them the benefit of the doubt. But there are times, too, when I'm not that magnanimous and I think, *"You asshole!"*

I've learned to remind people whenever I can, *never* to take anything for granted. Be grateful you can take a step. Be grateful you can see and hear. Be grateful you can take a shower without being terrified that you will fall stepping in or out of the stall. Be grateful you can stand in front of a stove and cook. Be grateful you can do the things you enjoy doing. Be grateful for your friends and family. No less important are our companion critters that help keep us sane with their unconditional love. Be grateful for any degree of what you consider normalcy in your life and, if and when you can, also be grateful for what you learn from the hard stuff. Just find every way you can to be grateful, period. By the way, don't be too critical of Facebook: it has saved my life. I may no longer have the luxury of seeing many friends "in 3-D," but my days and nights are flush with human contact, even if in virtual form, with an abundance of people I gratefully call friends. Some have come to Tucson and gone out of their way for us to meet. I ask you: how great is that?

One last thing: for heaven's sake, do not use a handi-cap parking place unless you have a permit. Someone like me might attack you with our wheelchair if you steal our precious spot.

~March 20, 2017~

About the Author

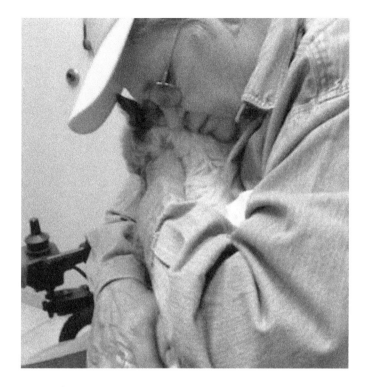

Lane Aldridge spent many of her seventy-five years as a teacher, an artist, and a traveler. She has been wheelchair bound since 2012 due to lumbosacral plexopathy, but that has only limited her ability to do a lot of the things she's always loved; it hasn't destroyed her passion for them, and it's given her enough time to put her memories to paper. She lives in Tucson with her beautiful Siamese cat, SyndiLou, and enjoys sharing life with friends around the world on Facebook. Lane's email address is inklings@cox.net.

CPSIA information can be obtained
at www.ICGtesting.com
Printed in the USA
LVHW030546030420
652112LV00002B/461